What They Don't Teach You in Law School

How to Get a Job

**The Six-Step Process for Landing a Great
Legal Job Even if You Don't Know
Where to Start**

Adam Gropper

Copyright © 2018 Adam Gropper. All rights reserved. No portion of this book may be reproduced mechanically, electronically, or by any other means, including photocopying, without written permission of the publisher. It is illegal to copy this book, post it to a website, or distribute it by any other means without permission from the publisher.

Adam Gropper

Arlington, Virginia

Adam@Legaljob.com

www.Legaljob.com

First Edition: February 2018

10 9 8 7 6 5 4 3 2 1

The materials contained herein represent the opinions of the author and should not be construed to be the views or opinions of the law firms, companies, or Federal Government with whom the author is in partnership or is associated, or by whom the author is employed.

Nothing contained in this book is to be considered as the rendering of legal advice for specific cases, and readers are responsible for obtaining such advice from their own legal counsel. This book is intended for informational and educational purposes only.

Praise for "What They Don't Teach You in Law School / How to Get a Job"

The advice is sound and the use of case studies involving schools from different tiers help illustrate its points in a very relatable way. —**Andrew J. McClurg, Professor of Law, Herff Chair of Excellence in Law, University of Memphis Cecil C. Humphreys School of Law and author of the bestselling law school prep book, 1L of a Ride**

A well-written book with compelling narrative examples and concrete advice that will help law school students find meaningful jobs upon graduation. —**Laura Rosenbury, Dean and Levin, Mabie & Levin Professor of Law, the University of Florida Levin College of Law**

The book was a remarkably easy and enjoyable read. It is going to help a lot of people who don't have the first clue where to begin finding a job outside of On-Campus Interviewing. —**Anthony D. Glosson, Associate, Drinker Biddle & Reath LLP**

A thought-provoking book that will make you a stronger candidate. —**Abraham Pollack, Associate Dean for Professional Development and Career Strategy, the George Washington University Law School**

The book is well-written and contains a lot of useful information much of which I utilized to get my job. —**Alex Scoufis, Attorney, Financial industry, self-regulatory organization**

This book is terrific. Very helpful to those looking for a job. —**Christopher H. Hanna, Alan D. Feld Endowed Professor of Law and Altshuler Distinguished Teaching Professor, Southern Methodist University Dedman School of Law**

The messages articulated, implicitly and explicitly, are sound. For instance, "choosing a major" really is vital outside of the biglaw OCI process. In addition, the book does a good job of addressing a common student impulse to keep all options open. Well done! —**Robert A. Cacace, Executive Director, Professional Development, Office of Career Strategy, Georgetown University Law Center, & Adjunct Professor of Law**

An inspiring book worth reading—with fresh insights and practical advice for those seeking to land their desired legal job. —**Jeffrey H. Paravano, Managing Partner, Baker & Hostetler LLP**

ACKNOWLEDGMENTS

There are several people that helped make this project possible, and I am pleased to have the opportunity to acknowledge them here.

Thank you to Howard. This book would not have happened without him. Howard is my mentor, coach, editor, sales and marketing guru, and publisher, all in one. He encouraged me to get going and held me accountable to stick to my plan. Perhaps most important, Howard taught me how to stop thinking and writing like a lawyer so that I could create an impactful and user-friendly book. I am very thankful for his guidance, wisdom, and friendship.

Thank you to my masterful editors, Yusuf and Safie, who were very patient throughout the multiple rounds and whose refinements greatly improved the book. I appreciate their contribution and assistance.

Thank you to my reviewers—Abe, Andrew, Alex, Chris, Gordon, Jeff, James, Laura, Rob, Roger, Tina, and Tony—for their helpful feedback and insightful comments which served to enhance the content and quality of this book. I am thankful for their willingness to help and take the time to provide their valuable input.

Thank you to my law student clients for the opportunity to partner on the path for securing their great legal job. Their stories, documented in the book, of setbacks and successes along non-traditional tracks will no doubt motivate and educate current students and demonstrate what is possible. I am inspired by their commitment, open-mindedness, and perseverance, and I am grateful for the chance to work with them.

Thank you to Amy, my wife and best friend, who has been so tolerant, encouraging, and supportive of this and so many other projects. She is the best thing that happened to me, and her presence and calming influence in my life helps keep me grounded and humble. I feel incredibly lucky to be with such a giving, wonderful person and companion.

Thank you to my young daughter Emma and toddler son Jack who are so enjoyable to be around and have been great teachers. Relevant to this book and dealing with potential employers, effective communication with my kids requires me to tune into what they want and why, to regularly confirm that I am on the right track, and to keep any explanations short and sweet. I really enjoy being their dad and appreciate their influence on some of the concepts presented.

Thank you to my mom who raised me, encouraged me to become a lawyer, and perhaps most relevant to this book, taught me the value of grit and never giving up. Mom's valuable advice and encouragement to keep going helped me through many rejections and ultimately put me in this position where I could offer information to others about how to succeed. I am proud to be the son of such an amazing and strong woman.

Thank you to my in-laws, Gigi and Pops, for their support and generosity. Their strong participation and assistance on the childcare front and with handyman projects freed me up to spend additional time polishing and perfecting this book. I feel privileged to have such decent, benevolent people in my life.

ABOUT THE AUTHOR

Adam Gropper is the founder of LegalJob LLC, a results-oriented coaching practice to which he brings expertise as a practitioner both as a former big firm tax partner at Baker & Hostetler LLP and a Legislation Counsel on the staff of the non-partisan Congressional Joint Committee on Taxation that helps Congress craft tax law.

Adam coaches open-minded, tactical-thinking law students interested in strategic support to identify their dream law job, create a clear plan to secure it, and competently execute the plan. Adam also helps highly motivated law firm associates advance to the top of their careers more quickly. Adam teaches them a unique way to think, act, react, and interact in a manner that enables them to provide superior service to partners and existing clients and also attract and cultivate new clients.

You can find Adam's insider tips and practical career advice for busy law school students and hard-working law firm associates at LegalJob.com.

Adam is the author of *Making Partner: The Essential Guide to Negotiating the Law School Path and Beyond (American Bar Association 2013)*. Making Partner provides guidance for maximizing performance while in law school, securing a great legal job, excelling as an associate, and moving on the fast track to making partner. Adam also wrote the introduction and contributed to the content of the *Vault Career Guide to Law* (Vault.com 2017). The Vault Career Guide to Law provides an insider's perspective on what's happening in the industry, what it takes to break in, and how to advance your career.

Adam is a licensed Certified Public Accountant and has a Juris Doctor, with honors, from the George Washington University Law School, a Master of Taxation from Florida Atlantic University, and a Bachelor of Science in Accounting, with honors, from the University of Florida.

TABLE OF CONTENTS

INTRODUCTION

Thinking Like a Lawyer

...may help you get through law school and pass the bar, but it may also hinder your efforts to identify and land a great legal job.

For a graduating law student, the task of securing a desirable legal job can be overwhelming. Now, more than ever, law students are trying to keep their heads above water and figure out what is expected of them. Not surprisingly, they worry that they will accumulate massive debt, waste precious time, and, in the end, fail to obtain a decent-paying legal job. All too often, that is exactly what they do.

There is plenty of helpful free information out there on such topics as how to study, how to think like a lawyer, how to read and outline cases, how to write, how to succeed at moot court, and so on. There is less guidance on the important question of how law school students and recent law school graduates should conduct a successful job search. This aim of this book is to fill that gap by providing interrelated career planning action steps. Following these steps should transform you into a stronger, more attractive applicant and put you on the path to obtaining your dream legal job.

What They Don't Teach You in Law School—How to Get a Job is a compilation of nearly 20 years' worth of advice and experience. It reflects the observations and feedback from recruiters and many potential employers, including partners, general counsels, and decision makers in top law firms and companies of all sizes, and people with hiring authority in Congress. The suggestions you will find here reflect takeaways from many lively discussions with law school professors, deans, and other administrators, and current and recently graduated law school students, including many students whom I successfully coached and mentored to help secure their dream legal job. In some measure, the advice is also based on my own experience at law school years ago.

An ambitious law student, I wanted to work at a top law firm. At the time, I had no idea that one of the shortest, easiest paths to full time employment at such a firm was to earn excellent grades as a first-year law student and then secure a summer job at one of those firms. More importantly, I had no idea how to prepare for exams or of the value of such resources as study groups. I ended up with mediocre grades and no clear path to the promised land of big firms.

When my law school's fall interviewing program process yielded only one interview and no call back, the career development office told me to rethink my plans. Professors, fellow students, and alumni also told me to lower my sights. I didn't listen. I thought there had to be another way. There was another way, and it is detailed in these chapters. For me, this strategy yielded three interviews and two big firm offers one month before graduation. I ended up with a position in a top firm that had rejected me on two previous occasions.

The fact that this strategy was successful should be welcome news for all of you who are not on law review, or are not attending a top 20 law school, or both. Of course, top grades and class rank still represent the most straightforward path, especially at non-elite schools, to landing a great legal job. But it is not the only path. The approach provided below has worked for students of high and low class rankings and those from all law school tiers.

◆ ◆ ◆

Obtaining an enjoyable legal job can be one of the most stressful tasks you will face as a law student. It is stressful, in large part, because one of the things law school doesn't teach you is how to "sell" yourself. More specifically, how to make potential employers see you as integral to achieving their objectives.

Law school teaches you a unique way of analytical thinking. This way of thinking is useful for lawyers grappling with legal issues, but it is often paralyzing when deciding what type of law you want to practice and how best to pursue rewarding career opportunities in that field. In this book, I explain how you can take off your law student hat and use a different approach when career planning which helps ensure that the extra thinking time is spent productively.

The book provides six steps that will help you identify your dream job, create a clear plan for securing it, and quickly and competently execute the plan.

In beginning this task, you need to switch your mindset from that of a law student seeking to be placed to one of a future employer seeking to fulfill its mission. If the employer is a law firm, for example, its mission may be to develop the people and resources necessary to deliver effective and unique legal services. Looking at your job search from this perspective, you must learn to ask yourself what you can offer, now or in the future, that will help your desired employer operate consistent with that mission. What is it that the employer is looking for? At a minimum, it is presumably interested in continuing to provide extraordinary client service while reaching (or exceeding) certain numerical targets. How would hiring you be helpful in meeting these goals? What else does the employer want or need?

Once you shift to viewing your job search from an employer's perspective, you are ready to take helpful, inspired action. This action relies on an entrepreneurial approach to your career planning, one that builds your brand with the aim of getting the job you want with the employer you want.

Your success in obtaining a desirable job will require more action than analysis, and more strategy than logical skill. This book will walk you through this shift in perspective and help you become comfortable with a proactive approach that supports the aim of creating multiple job opportunities.

What Is a "Great" Legal Job?

The description of a great legal job will be different for different people. For some, it may be a job at a top-tier firm. For others, it may be working for a small firm or a specialty firm. Some may favor working in the legal department of a major corporation. Others may have their sights set on working for a government agency. Working for a non-profit organization is yet another option.

The nature and size of the organization, the area of practice, the income potential, the opportunity for personal and professional growth, the working environment, and the opportunity for advancement are all elements that go into defining a "great" legal job.

You may already have a picture of *your* great legal job. If so, congratulations. Be forewarned, it will likely change over time. If you don't yet have that picture, that's okay. It will develop as you work through the six steps presented in this book.

Following is a list of those steps. They are the steps that I followed and that I advise every law student to follow in seeking a job. The rest of the book expands upon each step with examples that offer practical application. Note that many of the examples involve jobs with Biglaw firms and involve the tax law field, but these same steps have been used to successfully secure positions in a variety of practice areas in-house, in government, and at small law firms.

1. Commit to a Plan

Pick a system and follow it. Use the guidance outlined in the pages that follow to develop your own specific plan. As you follow it through, don't question whether you should be doing something more or something different.

2. Choose a Major

Choose a field of interest and perhaps a sub-specialty in an area in which you have some interest and where there is a demand. I'll show you how to go from having no idea what you want to practice to gathering sufficient information necessary to pick an area where your service could be useful in addressing the likely needs of prospective employers.

3. Network Effectively

When you meet with people to discuss your choice of major, to talk about job opportunities that exist in a particular field, or to pursue a job, be specific about what you want and how you think the other person might help. As you do this, show authentic interest in the other person's aspirations and challenges.

4. Think Like an Employer When Building Your Brand

Execute the three task items of earning good grades (especially in your major), obtaining relevant experience, and networking with the goal of bringing something uniquely valuable to employers. Also, create additional demand for your services by matching your brand to employer needs in your cover letter, your resume, and your 30-second commercial (a concise overview of the typical pains, challenges, and problems you can make disappear for people lucky enough to work with you).

5. Become an Expert on the Employer

Help the employer answer the question "Why should I hire you?" with the following steps: First, have a clear understanding of the employer's objectives and the resources needed to achieve those objectives. Second, demonstrate a deep, clear, and specific understanding of the employer. Third, articulate how hiring you will get the employer the results it wants more quickly and at a reasonable cost.

6. Focus on the Plan, Not the Outcome

Play the long game. Don't be distracted by apparent victories or apparent defeats. Everyone, including the top students in your class, is going to get rejection letters. Don't let it get you down when it happens. Don't dwell on either positive or negative thoughts. To prepare for the inevitable twists and turns of your job searching process, stay committed to your plan, be prepared to question your own assumptions, and be persistent.

◆ ◆ ◆

A set of questions to help you define a "Great" Legal Job and a template you can use to journal your weekly progress on each of the six steps identified in this book can be downloaded at www.LegalJob.com/Resources.

CHAPTER 1

Commit to a Plan

"Most people fail, not because of lack of desire, but because of lack of commitment."—Vince Lombardi

What can law students do to win competitive job offers upon graduation? They can create and commit to a plan. You'll learn why that's important in this chapter. In the chapters that follow, you will discover how to develop your particular plan.

In addition to GPA and class rank, what separates successful law students from others is that they are very clear on what they want and why they want it. Equally important, they are clear about how their own desires meet specific employer needs. They have a laser-like focus that allows them to articulate exactly how their background and experience will help their employers meet critical goals and overcome difficult challenges.

As a student, how can you achieve this level of clarity? Although some students know what they want to do at an early stage without much research or networking, most need to develop a plan and, more importantly, *commit* to following it. Such a strategy will remove the need for you to attend every networking event or to expend valuable time and energy on obtaining career planning advice from every alumnus possible. This book will help you create a plan that will allow you to quickly evaluate the value of proposed actions and proceed accordingly.

What should you include in such a plan? The best results are obtained from a thoughtful strategy, with a focus on action and thought. Such a plan will help you to become involved in activities that improve your understanding of possible areas of law on which to focus. When this is happening, your progress is assured. This progress is measured in baby steps rather than giant steps. Even if it appears that the plan is not working because the right outcomes are not obtained within the timeframe you envisioned, you must stay the course and follow through to completion. This commitment is the key to success.

Why Is Committing to a Plan Important?

Committing to a plan is helpful in two ways. First, with a plan you will have an answer to such persistent questions as, "Should I reach out to more people?" "Should I do it differently?" "Should I go to this event or to that event?" "Should I skip this networking event, so I can study?" "Should I reconsider my preferred practice area?"

Without a commitment to a specific plan, your "overachieving" tendencies may get in your way. When you are told that networking is crucial, you may be inclined to attend every networking event and reach out to as many alumni as possible for career planning advice. Sticking to your plan not only helps to keep you sane, but it also helps to prevent career planning from getting in the way of your studies.

Armed with a plan, you can focus your mind and relax, knowing you have a tried and true system in place for getting a job. When an event comes up, you will know whether you should attend because it will be clear if the function fits within your plan. You will go to events with a clear idea of what you are expecting to get out of them, therefore spending your time wisely. Moreover, you will be able to quickly measure your success at such events.

Once you have such a system in place, you won't randomly ask someone for coffee to "pick his or her brain." You will know exactly who you would like to spend time with, what you want, and how the person might be able to help. This will allow you more time to focus on your law school performance.

The second and more subtle reason for having a plan is that it will help you find the right time split between decision making and action. Law students generally spend way too much time on the decision-making process and not nearly enough time on implementation.

Having a plan in place allows you to more easily distinguish between the process that is required for providing good counsel to a client and the process that is required for making effective career decisions. When providing client advice, a due diligence, careful analysis, and cover-all-bases approach makes sense. When planning for your career, however, it is not necessary to analyze every possible iteration and downside risk of every decision.

As a law student, you may be inclined to spend lots of unnecessary and unhelpful time hemming and hawing before making a decision. Even after this decision is made, you are likely to proceed with caution, unsure whether your choice was wise and "correct." With so much brain power and energy devoted to the decision, there will be little, if any, gas left in the tank for action.

All that effort makes little sense because there is no such thing as a wrong decision. There is only poor or insufficient implementation once the decision has been reached. Having a plan that identifies the relevant considerations at each decision-making point helps to automate your process and keep you moving forward. So, if the decision you make doesn't work out, you make another one, and so on, and so forth.

With your mind's energy focused more on the process than the result, you will have less attachment to the outcome of each event. As a result, you will think less about whether you had a good day or a bad day. All you need to consider is whether you followed the process. You will commit to seeing the plan through even if it doesn't result in multiple offers immediately.

When Should You Create Your Plan?

The short answer is, "Sooner rather than later."

However, you can't create a plan until you have a target at which to aim. So, you'll need to have chosen a major or have a strong notion of which field of practice you want to pursue.

What Most People Believe, and Why It Doesn't Work

Upon hearing the advice I've just shared with you, most people respond with a question that sounds something like this one: "Should my path really be so scripted? My dad is a successful lawyer and he had no plan but was open to opportunities when they presented themselves. He tells me to prepare myself for anything by getting good grades and heavy lifting work experience, but not to be rigid and to let life happen. Whatever happens will be for the best, or because it was meant to be. And if I plan, I may limit myself to possibilities that I can't even imagine now. Isn't he right?"

Well, yes and no. Some people become successful without a plan. These people may not give very helpful career advice because they can't tell you specifically how they achieved success. They just got lucky. But for every one of those lucky folks, there are many others scrambling to find enjoyable legal work upon graduation. This is especially true now because the legal landscape has changed and continues to change. There is fierce competition due to fee-sensitive clients and the outsourcing of legal work as a result of technology and globalization.

That said, there are arguments on both sides about whether to plan. Although "Dad" would be right if he argued that you can't control life no matter how hard you plan, you can influence your experience. You might worry that by overplanning, you risk taking yourself out of the running for an opportunity in a practice area you may enjoy (but have not previously explored) or with an amazing legal employer you never considered. But are these reasons persuasive enough to have no plan? Remember that you can make necessary adjustments along the way.

Case Study: Sarah

Sarah got into a top 25 law school but had no real career plan. Her dad, a litigator for a large New York law firm, advised her to focus on her studies and do well, especially early on in law school, to increase her opportunities.

Fortunately, Sarah did well enough in her first year to secure a summer associate position at a large New York law firm in the summer following her second year. The firm did not assign summer associates to a practice group, so Sarah could work on a wide variety of projects including two matters with the tax controversy group. As both tax matters were at the IRS appeals stage, she was able to join the partners for meetings with the IRS appeals officers. Sarah enjoyed the varied aspects of these projects, including negotiations with the IRS, learning the clients' businesses, and gaining exposure to various tax laws. In one of the cases, she participated in the conclusion of the matter, which resulted in a favorable settlement for the client.

Sarah enjoyed the tax work so much that she enrolled in basic tax law for the fall semester of her third year. Soon after she began this class, the firm she had worked with offered her a full-time position. This was good news and a big load off Sarah's mind. However, the letter specified that she would be assigned to the antitrust litigation team. Sarah was surprised. She hadn't worked on any antitrust matters during the summer and had made a point to express how much she enjoyed the tax projects. Nonetheless, she decided to make the best of her position in a top law firm. Perhaps she would enjoy the antitrust work, even though she was unsure what it entailed.

Sarah did well in her tax law class, and in her spring semester, she enrolled in corporate tax, thinking the subject matter might be useful for her antitrust work. She achieved good results in that class as well.

When she began working for the firm, Sarah asked the head of the HR department if it would be possible to work on the occasional tax project if she ever had time. She was told that people could be very territorial about their associates doing work for other practice groups. Sarah decided not to make waves and work only on the matters she was assigned.

After two years at the firm, Sarah was unhappy. Most government antitrust investigations do not go to trial, and as a result, Sarah spent little time in court. Most of her time was spent on motion practice, digging through documents, and responding to government inquiries. The worst part of it was that she did not enjoy the subject matter. Sarah gave it one more year and then left the firm and traveled to her parents' house in Italy, where she spent several months trying to figure out what to do with the rest of her life.

If Sarah had followed the steps outlined in this book, putting together a clear plan before she began her summer clerkship, she might have learned more about the nature and day-to-day activities of both tax and antitrust practices and made different choices. The three years she spent working in a practice area she did not enjoy may not be helpful in terms of qualifying her for another firm job, particularly if she wants to try a new field such as tax law. With a plan in place, she might have insisted on working in tax law or held out for a different offer.

Case Study: Kevin

Kevin was a decent, but not stellar, night student at a second-tier law school. Kevin worked as an auditor for three years at a large accounting firm but was bored. He had a mentor, Paul, who was a senior attorney and partner at the firm who suggested that Kevin consider attending a first-tier local law school at night, achieve stellar grades, and put himself on a quick path for a summer associate position at a prestigious big law firm job, perhaps in tax, securities, or really any type of law where his accounting background would be a benefit. Kevin expressed some hesitation telling Paul that he was not completely sure that law school was the right decision. What if he invests all that time and resources and he cannot do better than his current job, or worse, he becomes undesirable altogether? Paul explained that, at least in his experience and in the experiences of folks he has mentored, the decision is less important than the act of committing. According to Paul, it was the commitment to a path, and all of its twists and turns, that opens up different opportunities. This advice resonated with Kevin as he realized his initial commitment to accounting led him to meet Paul, who was an amazing mentor.

So, Kevin took Paul's advice. He liked the idea of building upon his current experience while likely making more money, and potentially finding professional fulfilment. Unfortunately, the best Kevin could do was secure a spot on the waiting list at one of the top schools and after his first year, Kevin was just barely in the top 30 percent of the class, so transferring was not an option. After going through the fall interviewing program in the beginning of his second year, Kevin found himself not only with no big firm options, but no fallback options either. Kevin considered dropping out versus the prospect of adding to his sizeable loan balance with no obvious law job possibilities. His plan (or really Paul's plan) had failed. Kevin was at the wrong school with the wrong grades. Moreover, unlike some of his law school colleagues, Kevin did not have connections at big or even small law firms. Kevin was in a tough spot. But he did have Paul who, as the saying goes, had been there and done that.

So, he decided to seek Paul's guidance before quitting. Paul advised Kevin that all was not lost if he was prepared to be flexible and modify his plan. It may take him a couple of steps, but if he was committed it was likely that eventually he could end up at a big law firm. The new plan involved Kevin leveraging his current accounting experience into a government position, perhaps with the IRS, where he could get top-notch technical training. From there, Paul suggested that Kevin could eventually leverage his government experience and understanding of how the other side thinks into a position at a big law firm. Paul spoke from relevant experience as years ago he transitioned from his first law school job with the IRS into a large law firm.

Within two weeks of this conversation, and while he was still on the fence about continuing down another path that might not work, Kevin attended an alumni career event featuring representatives from four government agencies. One of the panelists, Lila, was from the IRS Office of Chief Counsel (basically the law firm for the IRS). Lila mentioned that her office had a summer internship spot available in its Honors Program. That position was highly sought after because, assuming there was sufficient funding and the summer experience went well, it would lead to an offer of full-time employment upon graduation with a three-year commitment to stay with the IRS. Right then and there, Kevin decided he would follow Paul's advice and try plan number two. If this worked out, he would quit his accounting job. When the panel concluded, Kevin introduced himself to Lila and asked her what the ideal candidate looked like. She explained that having some relevant experience and knowledge of what the office does were two pluses. Kevin asked if he could reference meeting her and learning this information in his application. She didn't seem overly encouraging or friendly, especially for an alumnus, but Kevin appreciated her information and permission to use her name.

Kevin applied and was granted an interview. Before the interview Kevin prepped with Paul who explained not only the substantive pieces of the job, but also structurally how the IRS Office of Chief Counsel interacts with the field and practice offices. Paul advised Kevin to emphasize his accounting methods experience because Paul knew that was an area that was needed at the IRS. Paul also suggested that Kevin articulate his deep understanding of what the day-to-day job looks like in terms of who he would be supporting. Kevin nailed the interview and got the job. In the end, the IRS didn't care that he wasn't in the top of the class or that he hailed from a second-tier law school. However, he was told that his application, given his mediocre numerical credentials, wouldn't have popped out without the head's up from Lila that his accounting methods experience may be particularly useful. You never know, Kevin thought! He didn't get "warm and fuzzies" from their interaction so he wouldn't have guessed that Lila would have done anything for him. Kevin was also told that he was picked out of hundreds of candidates because more than any other person, his knowledge of the mission and functions of the Chief Counsel's Office demonstrated a level of seriousness and commitment to tax that distinguished him from the other applicants.

The internship went well and Kevin ended up working there for 3.5 years until, following Paul's guidance, he left and landed in the tax group of a big law firm doing controversy work. Kevin's case for the law firm job was obvious. As he said in his cover letter, "Working at the IRS and being a CPA as well as an attorney, I speak the agency's language such that I may be able to help resolve audits of your Fortune 100 company clients quickly and favorably without expensive and time-consuming litigation." The law firm also didn't care too much about his class rank or that he hailed from a second-tier law school.

Kevin committed to a plan and took the long-term view. Like many law students from lower ranked schools, with less than stellar grades, or both, Kevin found himself with no job options after the fall interviewing program. He did not quit though. He sought help from someone who had done what he wanted to do, followed the advice, and ended up leveraging his government agency experience into his definition of a great legal job.

Planning for Letting Life Happen

The best solution is to commit to a plan while, at the same time, remaining open to all possibilities that come to you. How do you check both of these boxes? You create a plan that takes uncertainty into account, considering and identifying certain preferences in advance. You recognize that no matter how rigorously you have planned, life may bring you an opportunity you have not considered.

The plan for letting life happen is straightforward:

- Come up with a clear vision of the future. Decide who you want to help and what problems you want to solve.
- Determine the necessary steps to achieve this vision.
- Find someone to hold you accountable in following your plan.
- Follow the "Three Ps" outlined below to achieve a "let life happen" mindset.

A "let life happen" mindset allows you to remain flexible and prepared to consider any opportunity, including one that you may initially have perceived as undesirable. You achieve this mindset by identifying early on your preferences in the following areas, the Three Ps: the **P**eople you want to work with, the types of **P**rojects you want to work on, and the **P**rofessional development opportunities you seek.

The People

The people you work with are likely to have the strongest influence on your future professional development. Therefore, you will want a good connection with your fellow employees. Some people say the question to consider about a future colleague is whether the person would be good to "have a beer with." It is certainly worth considering social activities, alongside similar hobbies or backgrounds. However, in determining a potential fit, it may be more relevant to decide if you can see yourself comfortably spending long days with them (and sometimes long nights, depending on the employer and the project). If you like your colleagues, even the worst jobs will be more enjoyable. In deciding whether you have a good connection with potential colleagues, it is important to trust your instincts. How do you feel when you are around these people? Have any of the lawyers gone out of their way for you during the courting process? Perhaps someone has shown a sincere interest or been extra helpful in answering your questions.

The Projects

In assessing whether a potential employer will be able to offer you the substantive opportunities you need, consider the following questions: Will you be able to focus on an area of work you enjoy? Will you have the opportunity to take on significant responsibilities and to engage directly with clients? How many attorneys are practicing in the specific area on which you want to focus? Is there a system in place for assigning projects, and if so, how does it work?

The Professional Development Opportunities

To help evaluate professional development opportunities, consider the following questions: Does the potential job provide an opportunity for you to grow and develop, both as a lawyer generally and as a specialist in your practice area? Are there specific training programs offered at specific times during your career, or is it up to you to seek training? Has professional development been emphasized in your conversations with the employer? Will you be able to take on increasing responsibilities, such as interfacing with clients, mentoring younger attorneys, or taking on leadership roles? Does the employer encourage speaking and writing? Does the employer have a transition plan whereby senior lawyers or partners can train younger lawyers to eventually take a lead role on client matters? What is the general track for advancement? What are the alternative tracks?

What is the makeup of the group in which you will be working? It can be helpful to work with lots of junior attorneys in terms of going through life together at the employer and bouncing ideas off each other. On the other hand, your professional development opportunities may be increased at an employer with mostly senior people. Such a setup could allow you to work directly with senior attorneys or partners more often, offer greater client contact, and give you more opportunities to mentor younger lawyers. Different people will have different preferences in this area.

Case Study: Lisa

Lisa, who was in the top 20 percent of her class at a top 25 law school, did not know what type of law she wanted to practice. Fortunately for Lisa, she learned fairly early on in her law school career about the value of making and committing to a plan. Her plan involved spending time in activities that would help her better understand the nature of the legal work she thought she might enjoy. Because Lisa's father was an accountant at a large accounting firm, she had some familiarity with tax law, but it did not appeal to her. Her dad's lawyer colleagues touted its "puzzle-solving" aspect and suggested the field could draw on her undergraduate training and interest in economics. However, Lisa was more interested in learning about corporate law practice after talking with her dad's law school friend who described his mergers and acquisitions ("M&A") practice as fun and challenging with a certain uniqueness to each deal that keeps it interesting. That sounded neat to Lisa so she set out to learn more about what it was like to practice corporate law.

Lisa's research and discussion with practitioners led her to learn that a typical public M&A practice involved advising either the buyer or a seller in a transaction involving a public company. She further learned that it is not all interesting and stimulating work and can be very stressful especially for associates who have to spend hours reading and analyzing thousands of documents as part of due diligence reviews. Still, the work sounded interesting and the answer to one of her questions confirmed for Lisa that it was a field worth pursuing. Lisa asked about the characteristics of top M&A lawyers. She was told that lawyers who excel in the field generally have four things in common: 1) they understand what the client really cares about; 2) they strive to constantly produce excellent work; 3) they are intellectually curious; and 4) they are practical in the sense that they are problem solvers and can articulate the client's position in a clear and concise manner without sounding like a lawyer. One lawyer Lisa met with suggested that, in addition to reading the *Financial Times*, she take three courses in law school to confirm her interest and to improve her credentials, assuming she excels: securities regulation, corporate law, and business combinations or mergers. Lisa followed her advice and based on her strong performance in those classes, and the information she learned, Lisa set out to obtain her dream job: to become a big firm corporate lawyer.

In Lisa's third year, she found herself in the enviable position of having an offer to practice corporate law from two good firms. I'll call them Firm X and Firm Y. Firm X offered her a position to do corporate M&A work, which was her clear preference. Firm Y, on the other hand, offered her an opportunity to work in the private equity arena. Although Lisa's initial reaction was to accept the position at Firm X, she thought it might make sense to invest some time analyzing her two options. Lisa used the Three Ps as a framework for her analysis. At Firm Y, Lisa would be "stuck" servicing private investment firms for everything. The private securities offering piece of the practice interested her which is why she agreed to a second round of interviews. But many of the other projects—securities filings, investor reports and communications, incentive arrangements and regulatory and compliance issues—did not sound as desirable to her.

However, she was comforted on this front by her interviews with partners at Firm Y who seemed a bit more enthusiastic about their practice and role than the partners from other firms with whom she had met. Moreover, there were several pros about Firm Y which Lisa felt deserved consideration. Firm Y was rated one of the top firms for women attorneys. Its private equity group had five partners, two mid-level associates and one other first year associate. Lisa liked the manageable size and makeup of the group because she felt she would benefit from mentoring from both mid-level associates and partners, and she liked the idea of having a fellow associate with whom to share gripes. In addition, she was pleased to learn that her role as a young associate would not be much different from that of a senior associate or partner. So unlike the M&A practice which involved lower-level tasks, such as diligence, young lawyers in this practice got exposure to the whole picture, including drafting and negotiations.

Firm X, on the other hand, had a significantly smaller corporate group. There were no other entry level associates, one mid-level associate, and two partners. Lisa also learned that Firm Y encouraged associates to participate in article writing and seminars, while Firm X was silent on this type of activity.

Lisa went through the Three Ps for each firm.

The People—

Lisa asked herself if she could comfortably spend long days with the attorneys with whom she met. It was hard to know for sure as everyone was all smiles in the interview. On reflection, though, she felt a personal connection (in terms of shared interests) with two of the mid-level associates at Firm Y. Lisa then thought about whether any of the lawyers she met went out of their way for her in any manner during the courting process. At Firm Y, she thought the point of contact partner (who happened to be the head of the equity group and female) was extra helpful concerning information on timing and next steps and answering other lingering questions she had about the firm. She awarded one point to Firm Y.

The Projects—

Lisa considered whether she would have the opportunity to take on significant responsibility at each firm and if so, how soon. She also considered whether she would have the opportunity to focus on the area of work she thought she would enjoy.

Firm X offered Lisa the opportunity to work on large deals and concentrate her practice on advising on selling, combining, and acquiring businesses, which excited her. Both firms seemed to offer the same level of opportunities when it came to working on substantive client matters. One point for Firm X.

The Professional Development Opportunities—

Lisa considered which firm would provide the most significant opportunities for her to grow and develop. She noted that this area was emphasized in her conversations with Firm Y. In two of her interviews, they mentioned the fact that Lisa would be able to take on increasing responsibility in terms of type of work, interface with clients, mentoring younger attorneys, and leadership roles at the firm. She also noted that speaking and writing and developing her brand was brought up at Firm Y interviews and not mentioned at Firm X meetings. Another positive for Firm Y. However, Lisa recognized that as with any firm, getting the client's work done was still the priority for Firm Y. Accordingly, on her first pass, she gave Firm Y only half of a point for this category because she had no indication that Firm X would discourage her from speaking and writing and taking outside leadership roles.

On further analysis, Lisa learned that 25 percent of the leadership roles at Firm Y were held by women. That number was unusual for a big law firm, and Firm X had nowhere near this percentage of women leaders. As the head of the private equity group was female, Lisa felt very good about her growth opportunities at Firm Y. She increased its score in this category to a full point.

So, with the score of 2-1, Lisa ended up choosing Firm Y, even though she would be working on private equity rather than corporate M&A matters, her preference. Lisa is now a thriving second-year associate at Firm Y. By planning for letting life happen, with an up-front idea of her priorities and preferences, Lisa could weigh the variables and make a confident, informed decision about which firm was the better fit.

Takeaways

One key to securing your dream law job is being laser focused on what you want and why. Formulating and committing to a plan helps you achieve the kind of clarity you need to secure a great job offer.

If you are not clear about what you want and why, you could end up unhappy like Sarah, doing work you do not enjoy. On the other hand, if you commit to a plan that provides tools for identifying, evaluating, and securing various opportunities, including ones unforeseen, you could end up like Lisa, who chose a job outside her intended practice area because it fulfilled her remaining preferences. In the pages that follow, you'll learn how to build and execute such a plan.

♦ ♦ ♦

A list of additional questions to ask for each of the Three Ps can be downloaded at www.LegalJob.com/Resources.

CHAPTER 2

Choose a Major

"The risk of a wrong decision is preferable to the terror of indecision."
—Maimonides

You have decided to commit to a plan. Now it's time to choose a major.

Law school doesn't require you to pick the area of law you intend to practice in the form of a major. This may seem beneficial for those law students who are concerned about losing opportunities as a result of focusing on one particular practice. Yet there is a disadvantage to bear in mind. From day one in law school, students learn to identify and prepare for all possible likelihoods, a type of thinking that will serve their clients well. When crafting a career, however, it is impossible to identify and prepare for every possible contingency, many of which will be unidentifiable. It would be a waste of time to try.

The reality is that committing to a major enhances your opportunities. Once you decide what area of law to practice, you will be in a position to recognize and take advantage of education, work experience, networking and other opportunities that will help you secure employment in that field. Furthermore, employers are generally interested in law students who are focused and have tailored their law school careers toward gaining specific skills. They tend to prefer to employ people who have shown strong interest and commitment to particular practice areas.

As soon as you determine which practice area will match your interests and passions with the real needs of clients, you should pick a major (and, if possible, a sub-specialty) in that field.

This chapter describes the benefits of committing to a major and walks you through the steps involved in choosing a good match.

Stop Thinking Like a Lawyer

If you are like most law students, you probably spend a lot of time considering what type of law to practice. What should you pick? How do you make the choice? Have you even identified all of the possible choices? What if there are no jobs available in this practice area? What if you make the "wrong" decision and dislike what you do? Answering these questions is no easy task. Most likely, you don't have a vast knowledge base of information about the types and nature of legal job opportunities to help you out.

So, you hem and haw because law school teaches a valuable skill: how to think like a lawyer. This means that when faced with any challenge, you are likely to consider every possibility to exhaustion. As my wife would say, you "overthink it." You noodle over a myriad of "what-ifs." You approach every problem from all angles, examining all possible issues. You are cautious, pragmatic, and contemplative. These are helpful skills when analyzing legal issues and preparing for a law school exam. They are not very helpful when seeking to create demand for your services and separate yourself from the heavy competition. Quite the contrary, thinking like a lawyer may prevent you from becoming one.

So, how do you stop thinking like a lawyer? The first thing to understand is that when you are picking an area of focus or a particular employer, there is no such thing as the "right" decision. The key is to do whatever is needed to make a decision work for you, just as a businessperson would. As many successful entrepreneurs will tell you, success comes not only from thinking, but from motion and action.

The next thing to know is that although your mind may continually generate questions, you can control the level of focus and attention you give to these inquiries. Law students who shift their focus and time allocation from making decisions to implementing them tend to be most effective in career planning matters. Therefore, if you make what appears to be the wrong decision, such as choosing a major you are unsure about, but implement the plan well, you are more likely to be successful finding a job than someone who chooses what appears to be the right major but implements the plan badly.

Think of each decision point as containing ten parts. It often seems that nine parts are spent pondering the decision, leaving no gas in the tank for the final and most important part, executing the plan.

What if this formula were reversed, and you spent just one of the nine parts making the decision? Once the decision was out of the way, you could devote the remaining nine parts to its execution. You could redirect your energy to excelling in school by, for example, developing enhanced study habits that top students use to help ensure good grades. You could do everything possible to ensure the success of your decision by taking relevant classes, obtaining suitable job experience, and learning about the different opportunities in the field that corresponds to the chosen major.

So stop analyzing and start choosing. Then work toward successful implementation of your choice.

When should you make the choice? Once you identified a practice area you find interesting, established that you have the right skills for it or that you have a doable plan for obtaining the necessary skills, and talked to lawyers in the field, you are ready to choose. Remember, you can change your decision later and may do so several times.

Specialize, But Don't Overspecialize

Will specialization limit your opportunities or lower your value?

Some students are concerned that being characterized as a specialist may be damaging if they subsequently decide that they want to do something different.

Fear not. The choice of a major is informal, and it is possible to change to another major. Also, all is not lost if you spent a long time on the "wrong" major. You should be able to transfer to the new major some or all the skills or learning you have acquired. In this situation, your pitch to a prospective employer is that having researched the other area and spent time pursuing it, you have realized that your skill set is more suitable for the current area for reasons you specify.

But wait a minute. Shouldn't a good lawyer have at least a general understanding of different areas of the law? For example, if a new tax lawyer took nothing but tax courses before becoming a big firm associate, he or she might not be able to even spot a legal issue that is not tax-related when reviewing documents for a transaction. So, isn't the law student well advised to take a wide variety of classes so he or she can know enough to get another lawyer involved when necessary? In other words, isn't a good tax lawyer a good lawyer?

Also, can't the same point be made about lawyers in almost every field? A corporate lawyer should know something about corporate taxation as well as business associations and securities law, for instance.

The answer to all of these questions is "yes." At a minimum, you need to know enough to realize when you don't know enough. You can't ask for help from a lawyer in another field if you don't realize that there is an issue. If everyone was a single-minded specialist, a lot of problems needing attention would fall through the cracks—to the ultimate benefit of no one except the lawyers specializing in legal malpractice.

So, specialize, but don't overspecialize. Pick a major, take classes, and gain some experience in your major. Consider how the courses you choose could benefit future clients. If your school offers a concentration in a particular area, take advantage of the program and earn the credential. But you should also take a wide variety of courses in law school and broaden your horizons. For example, aspiring tax lawyers may benefit from taking courses in bankruptcy and vice-versa. Moreover, it is worth taking at least one course from each of the superstars on your law faculty, even if you never expect to make professional use of the subject matter, just to be exposed to great minds thinking great thoughts.

Case Study: Tim

An average law student from a top 25 law school, Tim is now a bored government worker. Although Tim heard about the importance of specializing in law school, he did not see this as an option. He did not know what he wanted to practice, nor did he want to spend time outside the classroom figuring this out. Moreover, he believed there was some value in being a generalist. Believing that all law school courses were likely to be of some professional benefit, Tim took a variety of courses, aiming to learn more about his preferences. Tim took the same generalist approach to work experience, and ended up with a hodge-podge of jobs — interning at a non-profit working on immigration law, serving as a Research Assistant to his local government law professor, and externing at a federal agency that administers and enforces civil rights laws against workplace discrimination. At this agency, he reviewed and evaluated cases that the local district offices were recommending for litigation. The agency experience sparked Tim's interest in litigation, so he decided to pursue a career in this field. He got close when a friend helped him secure an interview at a small firm that specialized in commercial and employment litigation. Tim interviewed well but ended up losing out to a person who had some commercial litigation background.

With one month until graduation, time was running out for Tim to get a job. When positions at various federal agencies were posted at his law school, he applied to all of them. Tim got a job at one of the agencies, where he now advises employees on conflict of interest statutes, ethics regulations, policies on the acceptance of gifts by the agency, and political activity rules. This is a far cry from litigation, and Tim is bored. To make matters worse, he feels that his boss continually changes policies by fiat, and he finds the work process painfully bureaucratic. The one silver lining is that the agency has about 12 other agencies under its purview, which cover all sorts of fields, including science, trade promotions, patents, and trade enforcement. As a result, Tim's generalist approach may be beneficial going forward. However, Tim is not gaining litigation experience, and the comparatively modest salary of a government worker is barely making a dent in his sizable college debt.

If Tim had picked a major early on, he might have found a job at a litigation firm, possibly the one that interviewed him.

A Solution that Works – Choosing a Major

"Okay," you say. "I am starting to see the benefits of picking a major, but how do I go about choosing one?" This is a good question asked by many law students. This section provides a road map for choosing a major.

How can you decide what area of law you will enjoy? If, like many law students, you are in law school because you couldn't decide on a career path in college, how is that going to change?

First, keep these points in mind: You may change your mind, and that is okay. I keep emphasizing this point in the hope that it will sink in. You may change your mind multiple times, and that is okay. You will likely change jobs multiple times, and that is okay.

The purpose of picking a major is to help put you on a path that will lead to multiple job opportunities. Most law students who have secured their desired job understand why they chose their major. This understanding came from meaningful research, asking hard questions, and connecting with helpful people, some of whom have obtained their preferred job.

The next section describes three action steps that help law students identify the major that makes sense for them: Take inventory, research possibilities, and talk with lawyers.

Take Inventory

Put some serious thought into the ways you like to spend your time. What are your hobbies? What types of books and magazines appeal to you? What are your particular skills? If you do not know, your friends and family probably have some thoughts, and there are a lot of resources out there to help you discover your strengths.

What do you like?

Perhaps start with a broad brush stroke. Ask yourself what type of lawyer you want to be, a transactional attorney or a litigator? As an example, do you want to handle mergers or litigation matters? Handling mergers may be desirable if you have dreams of working for a Fortune 100 company. Litigation matters often have you in a defensive posture, especially in private practice.

If there is no area that interests you more than others, consider such up-and-coming practice areas as digital asset planning, privacy law, non-traditional family practice, marijuana law, wine law, and robotics. These are growth industries that provide lots of job opportunities and have relative ease of entry, staying power, and wide geographic scope.

Similarly, for lucrative fields, you can look at regulatory practice areas that have high demand and multiple paths for obtaining a legal job. Tax is one example. Demand is outpacing supply in this area, and jobs are available at corporations, non-profit organizations, accounting firms, and law firms of all sizes. You could also work in government, for the IRS or Treasury, as a staffer for a member of Congress or one of the congressional tax writing committees. For other examples of regulatory areas with high demand, look at what is keeping Congress and the various Executive agencies busy. Securities, financial services, health care, and intellectual property matters all seem to be good candidates.

Where Would You Like to Work?

What is your ideal work setting? Do you want to live in a big city or a small town? Would you like to work at a big firm or a small one? How about government?

Take advantage of resources that provide an overview of the various legal settings for the top practice areas and those that explain the skills and training required and provide narratives from practitioners about their daily work life. The career services office at your law school can provide these resources at no cost.

After thinking about where you want to work, ask yourself what clients you want to work with and what problems they will have. If you want Fortune 100 Company CFOs and CEOs as clients, you will need to consider working in a big firm setting on such business and financial matters as antitrust, mergers and acquisitions, bankruptcy, and securities litigation. To excel in these areas, lawyers need both technical expertise and a strong understanding of the clients' businesses.

If that doesn't interest you, do you want to assist regular people trying to improve their everyday experience? If this is the case, consider a mid-size or small firm handling employment law, family law, or immigration law matters.

As you consider different practice areas, it will be helpful if you have something useful to bring to the area and more than a passing interest in the subject.

What Skills Are You Bringing?

If possible, build upon what you have in terms of education, background, or experience. If you have a degree in electrical engineering, for instance, you may add a lot of value up front as an intellectual property lawyer. Your strong technical and analytical skills will help you to understand client inventions, knowledge that is beneficial when it comes to obtaining and enforcing patent protections and navigating licensing opportunities. Similarly, people who are fluent in foreign languages or have ties to foreign countries have a leg up in terms of hiring by any law firm that engages clients or adverse parties from different cultures and language groups. In the same vein, prior work experience is desirable in that it could provide an opportunity to acquire skills relevant to certain practice areas.

As you consider the kinds of clients you want to help, note what interests you. Then ask yourself what experience you have with those clients and their industries. Consider which area of law is most relevant to the items you have identified.

What are the issues that people working in these industries spend their time thinking or worrying about? Are these issues the type on which you want to spend your time? Do you have innovative ideas relating to these issues or the industries generally?

What about your background or interests makes you well-suited to work in these industries or with these clients? Consider these questions:

- What are you offering that is unique?
- How and why is it unique?
- How would it help the prospective employer from day one?
- Why are you the right person to work in this area?

27

- Who else thinks you are qualified?
- What do you still have to learn about this area, and are you open to learning it?

Research Possibilities

Once you have taken inventory and have a couple of practice areas in mind, you are ready to do some meaningful research. Again, it might make sense to start with areas with high demand and low supply. High-demand areas are active and constantly changing. Tax is a good example both on the demand side and the supply side. The demand is high because constant changes to the law increase the need for technical tax lawyers. The supply is low because of the disproportionate amount of senior folks practicing in the area.

Technology is another area where demand outstrips supply. Technological advances have given rise to opportunities to specialize in areas such as intellectual property, software and business method patents, and privacy. In the area of privacy law in particular, demand has risen as recent high profile security breaches, personal identity thefts, and data thefts have led businesses to prioritize safeguarding customer and business information.

Keep abreast of current events that relate to the passage of new federal or state laws, particularly major legislation. Areas of the legal profession that frequently feature in the news are tax, health law, and securities.

The newspaper is a good introduction to current affairs, but industry periodicals, such as *The American Lawyer* for top law firms and *The Champion* magazine for criminal defense, can provide a more substantial review of topics.

Once you have set a target, or perhaps several targets, dig deeper into topics that interest you. Find out what lawyers who practice in particular areas are reading. Your professors or your law school's career services office may help you in this regard. Use this research to help you pick one or two subject areas or niches within a large practice area.

Finally, once you have chosen an area or areas, and perhaps a subject within the area, find out where this type of law is practiced. This may be at government agencies, law firms, non-profit organizations, and large or small companies. Find out if there are places in the country where these jobs are more abundant. Again, your career services office and your professors may be helpful.

Talk with Lawyers

When your research is complete and you have identified an area, you are ready to talk with people who practice in this area. You can discuss their career path and how they spend a typical day. Contact information will be available through your career services office or on social media. If possible, focus on people with whom you have something in common, such as the same hometown. More information on this strategy can be found in Chapter Three.

When meeting lawyers, ask them what they find interesting about their job and what skills are required to succeed. Start out by approaching the leading players, who may be more likely to meet with you if you ask their opinion on hot topics in their area. Note their credentials to help determine what about their background and experience qualifies them for the job. Later, during interviews with potential employers, you will be able to use your meetings with these lawyers to demonstrate your knowledge of the field.

Demonstrate a Commitment to Your Chosen Area

By now you should appreciate the importance of picking a major. You will be able to identify what you bring to the table and learn about the different practice areas that interest you. How do you put this preparation to work? How do you show an employer that you have chosen a major?

You demonstrate commitment by taking relevant classes, writing about hot topics in the area (including on social media), and obtaining useful work experience.

If you're a member of a journal that has a writing requirement, put together a thoughtful, well-written and researched case note or comment (or an article if you have graduated) on a current topic of interest in your major. For topic ideas, consider asking for recommendations from a law professor in the field related to your major. Also consider asking that professor if he or she would be willing to review your draft and provide feedback. Obtaining and incorporating comments further demonstrates your commitment to the practice area and will likely improve the writing, thereby increasing your attractiveness as an applicant.

Your major should be in an area that has at least two or three classes available. Some examples of possible majors include intellectual property, tax, corporate law, family law, litigation, and health law. Ideally, the major should build on previous work experience, as discussed above. You should pick courses that are directly on topic and courses that complement the area. For example, if you want to specialize in corporate law, take courses in corporations, securities regulation, venture capital law, and takeovers, but also consider complementary classes such as corporate tax and bankruptcy. Perform well in these classes so you can demonstrate to potential employers that you excel in the areas in which you will be working.

In addition to taking classes relevant to your major, you should grab any opportunity to write articles relating to your chosen area, especially on hot topics. Law professors are good sources of ideas and information to use in such articles.

As discussed above, it is also helpful to gain work experience in your major. Take a job that involves substantive legal work. Find out before you take the job what you will be doing and to whom you will be reporting. If possible, talk with people who did the job before you so you can get a true sense of what is involved.

Finally, take part in other activities that will demonstrate an interest in your chosen area. These activities might include entering a writing competition, participating in moot court, serving on the editorial board of a journal, starting a blog or commenting on existing blog posts, contributing to a relevant LinkedIn group, submitting comments in response to proposed government regulations, serving as a research assistant to a professor, or securing related credentials such as the patent bar for intellectual property law or the Certified Public Accountant designation for tax law.

Case Study: Trey

The case of Trey, a transfer student from a top 50 law school to a top 20 law school, demonstrates the benefits of picking a major. Trey had excellent grades at his first law school. Because he transferred, however, he was unable to participate in the new law school's fall interviewing program and, consequently, had no job prospects. Trey had worked as a freelance web developer before law school and knew he wanted to practice in an area that utilized these skills.

Trey did some research and learned that privacy law and communications law (as it deals with the internet) both have issues that intersected with his passion and experience in technology. He had initially decided on a combined major of privacy and communications law, but before finalizing, he thought it would be best to meet with some lawyers practicing in those two fields to confirm his interest.

Trey asked his career center for assistance and obtained the names and contact information of the major players in this space. He reached out to six people with whom he had something in common — they all had a technology background. One person, a privacy lawyer at a big firm, replied to his e-mail and was willing to meet. In his e-mail, Trey had asked the lawyer his view on a specific hot topic in the cyber security area. This topic concerned the issue of whether U.S. law could be interpreted to allow a private sector actor to respond to an intrusion by hacking the hacker in return. The lawyer shared his view on the issue, and Trey enjoyed his meeting and felt that his privacy major was solid. He didn't get much confirmation on the combined major with communications law, given that the lawyer did not practice in that area. However, the lawyer then connected Trey with his contact at an agency that regulates interstate communications. Through that second meeting, Trey was able to determine that his combined major choice made sense and that the areas were complementary. Equally as important, Trey leveraged that contact into a law clerk position for one of the agency heads. At the agency, Trey was exposed to a variety of legal and policy issues relating to its oversight of television, wireless, satellite, and other communications services. He later complimented this experience with a position at a non-profit technology think tank, where he worked on privacy, free speech, communications law, and cybersecurity.

In his third year of law school, Trey reached out to his big firm privacy lawyer contact to ask if he knew anyone that might benefit from his experiences. The partner was receptive and immediately referred him to a partner at another big firm. Impressed by the breadth of Trey's experience, this firm made room in its incoming associate class, even though it was full. Trey was hired to assist clients with a range of privacy, communications, and regulatory compliance matters. When asked how he was able to land a big firm job despite missing the fall interviewing program and transferring from a lower-ranked law school, Trey pointed to his focus on privacy and communications law and early selection of preferred practice areas.

Takeaways

If you approach your choice of major like a lawyer—90 percent analysis, 10 percent action—you may not make much progress and could end up like Tim, who deferred his decision and is now bored at his job. Instead, follow Trey's approach. He landed a lucrative and interesting big firm job after taking inventory, researching possibilities, and talking with lawyers in the two practice areas he was considering. This approach helped Trey to make an informed choice that matched his interest and experience with the needs of an employer.

♦ ♦ ♦

A tool that will give you additional guidance on choosing a major can be downloaded at www.LegalJob.com/Resources.

CHAPTER 3

Network Effectively

"The best way to succeed is to have a specific intent, a clear vision, a plan of action, and the ability to maintain clarity." —*Steve Maraboli*

In the previous chapter, I advised you to talk with practicing attorneys before finalizing your choice of major. Discussions with practicing attorneys can help you learn about the kinds of job opportunities that exist in a field, and even about specific positions. This chapter provides advice on how to obtain those meetings and get the maximum value from them.

Why Is It Important to Meet with Practicing Attorneys?

Hearing someone discuss his or her experiences in a specific area will help you confirm whether the field is right for you. At these meetings, you can learn what practicing attorneys do, what they find interesting or challenging about their jobs, and what skills are required to succeed.

In addition, in future meetings with potential employers, you will be able to reference these earlier meetings, illustrating your awareness of the issues that arise in these areas. This will help you demonstrate the relevance and usefulness of your background and skills in helping clients obtain desired solutions.

What Should I Ask?

Law students tend not to generate meaningful results when networking. This outcome is usually because they are not specific about what they want and how the other person might be able to help. For these reasons, law students trying to arrange such meetings tend to be even less successful than telemarketers, who have a one-in-ten success rate. Worse, many law students do not even try. This lack of effort may be because they do not know what to ask.

One good question to ask is how the practicing attorney ended up in his or her job. This will give you a sense of the thought process that leads one to choose a practice area. It doesn't matter if you are not interested in the specific area in which the person works. The process he or she followed to achieve that position may help you to evaluate different possibilities. Later, when you are interviewing, you might be able to use this information when articulating substantive reasons why you are interested in practicing a particular area of law.

Another question to ask a practicing attorney is who else it would make sense for you to meet. In this way, even attorneys whose insights will be of limited value may provide helpful contacts.

Here are some other items to explore when meeting attorneys:
- Which of their qualities and skills make them effective in their practice areas?
- What kinds of experiences and background would be most helpful to excel as a lawyer generally and in the practice area specifically? What classes should you take? What kind of work experience is valuable? In what law school activities (e.g., moot court, journal) should you participate to complement your work experience and the course curriculum?
- Is there anything they find particularly challenging about the practice?

Among the many opportunities available for law students to network are with alumni, participants in career panels hosted by the law school, and family friends. The professors at your law school and those involved with legal clinics may also provide helpful guidance on different practice areas or suggest whom you should consult.

To connect with alumni, ask the career development office to provide you with a list of 10-15 attorneys with whom you have something in common. Common elements can include undergraduate school, law school, major, hometown, previous work experience, shared hobbies, practice area, or some similar match with background or culture. Start with the attorneys with whom you have the most things in common. Contact them to learn how they ended up in their chosen legal field. Keep in mind that many people may refuse to meet you or not respond to your e-mails. That is okay. The one person who responds and meets with you may be all that you need.

When Can Networking Be Helpful?

Law school stresses the benefits of networking to help you get a job. It is true that networking can be helpful, especially for folks who are clear and specific about what they want and demonstrate a curiosity in others. However, ambitious law students may think they have to network all the time to be successful. As a result, they might burn out before meeting anyone who could really help them along their career path. To avoid this problem, consider the responses provided by former law students (who landed their desired job) when asked to identify the situations where they got the best results from networking. The top three responses were: 1) to learn more about a certain practice area, 2) to discuss general job opportunities available in a certain practice area, and 3) to obtain employment in a certain practice area.

Meeting with Lawyers to Learn More about a Particular Field

In the case study below, Austin reaches out to attorneys to learn more about tax law.

<u>Case Study: Austin</u>

Austin was looking for help in picking his major. He was interested in exploring tax law, but he hadn't narrowed down which type of tax law. To learn more about the field generally, he sent an e-mail to four senior international tax practitioners. This e-mail was a short message introducing himself, describing his background, and asking if they would meet for coffee to discuss his tax career path. One of Austin's good friends, Joe, was a family friend of one of the practitioners, Juan. Joe had no issue with Austin name-dropping and Austin was excited about the prospect of meeting with him.

Three weeks passed, and Austin had received no responses, not even from Juan. Confused by his zero-hit rate, Austin asked Joe whether it was possible to find out why Juan had not responded. Joe complied and forwarded the e-mail response from Juan.

> Hi Joe,
>
> I apologize for not getting back to your friend and for taking a bit to get back to you. I have been overseas at a client site for the past month, and I am just now getting my head above water. Your friend's e-mail came at a crazy time for me, but it also went to the bottom of my pile because it was somewhat unclear about what he wanted. It sounded like he is looking for a job? The firm has filled its summer class, so I don't know that there is anything I can do for him. Sorry, I couldn't be more helpful.

Austin was surprised at this response. He didn't think it sounded like he was looking for a job, and he thought Juan would have agreed to at least a brief meeting, especially given the Joe connection. He wondered whether all tax types were equally clueless and unwilling to help young people.

While we don't have Austin's e-mail, it seems reasonable to assume from Juan's response that Austin didn't put much time into thinking about what would motivate the practitioner to respond. Austin's e-mail was probably very general and did not provide specific details about what he wanted and how Juan could help. Here is an approach that might have yielded Austin a more favorable response.

> Hi Mr. Gonzales,
>
> I am Joe Summers' friend, and I am a second-year law student in the process of narrowing down my selection of possible practice areas upon graduation. I'm not looking for a job at this point, but I am interested in pursuing the field of tax law and specifically international tax.
>
> To help confirm my decision, I am hoping to learn about your career path and have a brief discussion with you at your convenience about current tax law issues in this space. For example, I am interested in your opinion on the current repatriation tax holiday proposals being floated by some members of Congress. Do you believe a mandatory tax on these earnings at a low rate makes sense from a policy perspective given current law, which provides for temporary deferral until the funds are brought back to the U.S.?
>
> I believe your firm represents several multi-national companies that this proposal could affect (and so I also understand if you prefer not to comment). Thank you in advance for any time you can spare to meet.

While there is no guarantee that Austin will receive a response, at least he has attempted to demonstrate, with the use of a provocative question, a sincere interest in the practitioner and his opinions. Now the meeting is not just about Austin and his career path. Note that this e-mail is specific about what Austin wants and how the attorney might help. He also makes it clear that he has done more than cursory research into the type of clients the attorney helps.

Meeting with Lawyers to Discuss Job Opportunities in the Field

In addition to learning what lawyers do in different practice areas, you may find it helpful to understand the various opportunities that exist in the field. Then, later, when meeting with potential employers, you can use this information to explain why, after considering the different opportunities, you believe your interests, skills, and experience are most suited for the specific position for which you are interviewing.

Case Study: Trevor

Trevor chose tax as his major. He made this choice because he had an undergraduate accounting degree and no strong interest in any particular area. Trevor did some basic preliminary research and discovered that two options he had upon law school graduation were working for a law firm or working for an accounting firm. To help him evaluate these options, he reached out to a senior transactional tax practitioner at a law firm with the following e-mail:

> My name is Trevor Mahoney, and our law school provided your name as an alumnus who may be willing to meet to discuss what it is like to practice tax in a law firm. I am a 2L interested in pursuing a career in tax law. If you are up for talking, could you please provide a couple of good dates and times for lunch over the next couple of weeks?

Thank you in advance for considering, and I look forward to speaking with you.

Unsurprisingly, Trevor did not receive a response to his request. While we do not know the reason for the lack of response, the e-mail request was not as effective as it could have been. Trevor was not very clear about the information he was seeking. For instance, he didn't say he wanted to meet to compare the practice in the two different settings: accounting firms and law firms. Furthermore, as with Austin, Trevor did not seem to put much thought into what would motivate a busy attorney to respond. Here is one approach that may have yielded Trevor a positive response.

> Hi! My name is Trevor Mahoney, and our law school provided your name as an alumnus who has offered to assist students considering a career in tax law. I am pursuing a career in tax law, and I am in the process of deciding whether to target law firms or accounting firms or perhaps both. I have heard that much of the sophisticated tax planning may be moving to the accounting firms. If you are comfortable sharing, I would be interested in learning your perspective and your take on possible future changes in the field. Please let me know if there are any dates and times that are convenient for a short call.

With this approach, Trevor thoughtfully keys in on an issue likely to be of interest to the attorney. Now, the meeting is not just about Trevor. He is also mindful of the attorney's time and very clear concerning the nature of the help he is seeking. A brief meeting or phone call is much easier to secure than a lunch meeting. With these tweaks, he would have a greater chance of receiving a response. Note that both e-mails mention that they went to the same law school. It is important to reference this connection.

Meeting with Lawyers to Obtain Employment

This type of networking is the one law students tend to dread the most. Requests for meetings of this kind also achieve the worst success rates. Consider the case studies of Jill and Remy below and the different results obtained in each.

Case Study: Jill

Jill was a 2L in the top third of her law school class. Her performance in her first year was mediocre, so she didn't get many bites from employers in the fall interviewing program. In the first semester of her second year, however, she earned excellent grades in classes that included corporations and securities law. As a result, Jill still had dreams of working for big law. She reached out to the career office at her law school for the contact information of alumni practicing corporate law at local law firms. Jill received three names and sent the following e-mail to one of the practitioners.

> Hi, my name is Jill Powers and our law school shared your name as someone who may be willing to meet for coffee to discuss your career path. And I thought it would be fun to share Evansville stories; it was a great place to grow up and my family is still there. Could you please let me know if you have any availability to meet briefly over the next couple of weeks?

This was not bad as far as e-mails go. Jill did a nice job of referencing the hometown she shared with the contact. As an incentive to meet, however, this is a little light. At a minimum, Jill needed to be clear about what she was requesting and to demonstrate some interest in the practitioner and his or her practice.

In contrast, consider Remy's approach.

Case Study: Remy

Remy was also a 2L in the top third of his law school class. Because he wasn't sure whether he wanted to work for government or a law firm, he didn't participate in the fall interviewing program. In his second year, Remy learned about an international law firm with a large presence in France, his home country. As one of the major practice areas of the firm was employment and labor law, he decided to take a class in the area and see if he liked it. Remy ended up doing well and enjoying the class, so he decided to pursue employment with that firm.

Remy consulted with his career office and learned that a law school alumnus from the firm was due to speak on a career panel hosted by the school. During the panel, three labor and employment law attorneys from different law firms would be discussing their experiences working for those firms. Remy consulted his professor about possible hot topics he could raise with the panelists. His professor suggested reviewing recently published Labor Department guidance concerning whether workers should be classified as employees rather than independent contractors. Remy looked up the guidance and jotted down some potential questions to ask.

When the audience was asked for questions, Remy raised his hand, and directed his question at all of the panelists. He said: "Hi, I'm a 2L interested in practicing labor and employment law. I read the recent administrative guidance dealing with employees who are misclassified as contractors. It doesn't seem like the agency has provided a new test but rather is just clarifying its view that most workers are employees, not contractors. Is that how you see it? And how are you advising your clients in relation to this issue and the potential exposure for unpaid wages, damages, interest, and penalties?"

Home run. Each panelist basically agreed that the test was not new and had a slightly different approach to dealing with the guidance. Two of the panelists, including his target, noted that Remy had a "good question" and a "good observation." Remy stayed after the panel and introduced himself to the alumnus panelist. Here's how that discussion went.

> **Remy:** Hi, thanks for taking the time to speak to us. I enjoyed the panel.
>
> **Alumnus:** It was my pleasure. You asked a thoughtful question. Not many law students are up to date on the latest DOL interpretations.
>
> **Remy:** Thanks. I'm interested in working in the area at a big firm. I took Labor Law and did well.
>
> **Alumnus:** Well, unfortunately I think our firm has filled its summer class, but shoot me an e-mail because I may know of another opening at a firm in town.
>
> **Remy:** Thanks for the opportunity. I will.

The following day, Remy sent the panelist this e-mail:

> Hi,
>
> My name is Remy Dubois. We met at the career panel you participated in at our law school. Thank you again for doing that. Everyone got a lot out of the panel.
>
> You mentioned that you may know of a job opportunity at another firm. I'm interested in talking with you further about this position, if you can find time in your busy schedule.

Also, if you are open to sharing, I would love to know your perspective on the type of candidates who were successful in obtaining a job at your firm and excelled once there. With your permission, I intend to pass along what you share with the career office so that other job seekers may benefit and so that the school can refer high-potential candidates to your firm in the future.

If helpful, I can come to the firm in the early a.m. or after hours, whatever is most convenient.

Remy received the following response one week later.

Hi Remy,

Thanks for the note. Would you have any interest in interviewing with our firm? It turns out one of our summer associate candidates changed her mind and will not join us this summer. As a result, we have a potential spot open.

Remy ended up interviewing with the firm, including with the panelist, who, as it turned out, was also the head of the Labor and Employment group. After a productive and enjoyable experience as a summer associate, Remy accepted an offer of full-time employment with the firm.

Remy followed a very different approach to Jill, and it paid off. His preparation for the panel helped him to come up with a thought-provoking question relevant to the practice. Thus, he demonstrated a sincere interest in others. When making his request, he was up front and clear about what he wanted to know. Furthermore, he was shrewd to mention passing along the advice to the career office, given that by participating in the panel, the alumnus had already demonstrated an interest in helping fellow alumni.

Takeaways

The experiences of Austin, Trevor, and Jill show that networking for any purpose can be a most unpleasant and unproductive activity for law students. Those three students went about networking in the traditional way and received no response. This poor result was probably obtained because they were not clear about their purpose and did not demonstrate an interest in the opinions, career path, and concerns of others.

As Remy demonstrated, on the other hand, there is another way that is less painful and yields results. Remy's success was due to the following techniques: First, he researched the area. Then, he found an in-person opportunity to connect. Next, he tuned into several issues of interest to the attorney. Notably, he was up front and clear about what he wanted and how the attorney could help. Finally, he was mindful of the attorney's time and busy schedule.

♦ ♦ ♦

A list of questions that have yielded useful information during interviews and other employment-related discussions and samples of effective networking request e-mails can be downloaded at www.LegalJob.com/Resources.

CHAPTER 4

Think Like an Employer When Building Your Brand

"The more I help others to succeed, the more I succeed." —Ray Kroc

In the first three chapters, I talked about the advantages of committing to a plan, choosing a major, and networking effectively. In this chapter, I will show you how to communicate your value to your desired employer. You will need a clear idea of what you are bringing to the table and the ability to demonstrate that you have the right skills, experience, results, and habits.

When they ask how to obtain their desired job, most law students are told to earn good grades, obtain relevant experience, and network as much as possible. This advice is not wrong, but it is incomplete. It fails to explain how you can make yourself stand out to potential employers. To stand out when looking for a job, you need to think like an employer. You need to create a demand for your services from the employer's perspective.

If you have followed the advice of the second chapter, you will have chosen your major at an early stage. By excelling in classes relevant to that major, you will show future legal employers that you are likely to excel as an employee. Moreover, you will demonstrate a commitment and interest in the area that will distinguish you from your competitors.

This chapter provides guidance on how to market yourself in a manner that considers the needs and objectives of a potential employer and its clients. It provides tips for refining your resume, your cover letter, and your "30-second commercial" so they match your brand to these needs.

Why It's Important to Market Your Brand to an Employer Need

You're interested in being a lawyer, not a salesperson. So, why all this talk about marketing and branding?

Now more than ever, the practice of law is a service *business*. Certain aspects of law jobs—attracting the interest of legal employers, providing superior service to existing clients and partners, and attracting new clients—require a different set of skills and mindset than you would use to analyze a legal problem. This dynamic is true whether you are seeking to work at a law firm, for the government, or in-house at a company. In any of these areas, job candidates must understand and employ certain business principles to maximize their opportunities. To excel in school and in practicing law, you needed issue spotting and critical thinking skills. To excel in the legal job market, you need a different set of skills.

Law students and lawyers tend to think of themselves as different, smarter, or more special than others. When it comes to creating a brand that can be successfully marketed to an employer's needs, however, you will need the same steps and mindset required in obtaining any job. You need to demonstrate in clear and specific ways how your background, knowledge, and experience position you to help your ideal employer solve its problems and obtain its desired outcomes.

An important concept to keep in mind is that you are not your potential employer. Before creating your brand and targeting your employer, you must switch your orientation and focus from you to that employer. *You* may care where you went to school, where you are from, and how much you have done in your life. But *your potential employer* only cares about how you can help solve its challenges and achieve the outcomes it desires.

The adjustment in point of view required is demonstrated in the well-known experiment in which a three-year-old child discovers that a familiar crayon box contains candles. The three-year-old is asked what his friends will think is in the box before they look inside it. The three-year-old mistakenly assumes that his friends will know it has candles inside, just as he does. He makes this assumption because he hasn't yet learned that others have beliefs and perspectives different from his own. When the same experiment is conducted with a five-year-old child, the five-year-old predicts that his friends will be fooled, just as he was, and believe that the box contains crayons. The five-year-old understands that others, lacking his knowledge, will see things differently.

To obtain a legal job, law students need to step out of the mentality of the three-year-old in the experiment and refine their thinking to that of the five-year-old.

How Do I Market My Brand to an Employer Need?

Before marketing your brand, you first need to know your ideal employer's challenges, the impact of these challenges, and the outcomes the employer desires. As a preliminary matter, you need to understand the employer's culture, its history, and the types of clients it represents. To obtain this knowledge, you need to do more than scan the employer's website. You may need to talk to an employee, a client, an associate, or a partner. Other steps that can be taken to gain a deeper understanding of the employer are detailed in Chapter Five.

Once you have become an expert on your ideal employer, your mission is to demonstrate that expertise. Your resume, cover letter, and 30-second commercial can provide details on how you can make an immediate contribution to the employer and help solve its challenges. Your long-term objective is to position yourself in such a way that the employer is convinced that it needs you on the team.

Branding: What Works and What Doesn't Work

The case studies below illustrate the benefits of thinking like an employer when creating resumes, cover letters, and 30-second commercials.

Case Study: Natasha's Resume

Natasha was a 2L in the top 25 percent of her class at a top 25 law school. In her first semester, she participated in the fall interviewing program with the goal of securing a summer associate position in a corporate law practice. Natasha applied to seven firms, but the only interview offer she received was for the out-of-state offices of just one of those firms, a position in which she had little interest. Natasha could not understand why her resume did not gain more traction. Her grades were not stellar, but she thought they were good enough given her school's ranking.

Natasha's mom's neighbor and friend, Trish, who was the head of human resources at a top law firm, offered to review her resume and meet with her to give her some advice. Below is a transcript of that meeting.

> **Natasha:** Hi, Ms. Baker. Thanks for offering to meet and help me figure out why I got so many rejections.
> **Trish:** My pleasure. Please call me Trish. Natasha, may I be completely honest with you?
> **Natasha:** Ah, okay.
> **Trish:** The two things our attorneys care about most are law school ranking and grades. In these categories, you are not breaking any records. Agreed?
> **Natasha:** Well, I guess I thought top 25 in both categories is not too shabby. But okay, so are you telling me I have no chance at a top law firm with my grades and school ranking?

Trish: No, Natasha, I'm not saying that. I'm saying most of our summer associates are from top 10 schools in the top 10 percent of their class. Not all of them have those credentials, though. What the rest of them have in common is some relevant work experience or other intangibles, such as fluency in a foreign language, which can benefit the firm's practice in some way. We don't spend a lot of time reading and interpreting resumes. So, to show us you have this intangible quality, it is best to provide a concise, easy-to-follow explanation of your roles in various projects and solutions achieved.

Natasha: Okay. I thought I did that.

Trish: Well, I'm not sure if you did. My quick, ten minute—and, believe me, we typically spend half that time—impression of your resume is... (she paused). Okay to be blunt?

Natasha: Yep.

Trish: Okay, I thought your resume was too long. Two pages are too much for us to read. Also, it seems to be written from your perspective – your experiences and accomplishments – and not from the perspective of the person reading it, who wants to know what you can do for the firm... In some places, you went into more detail than I thought was necessary and in other places, I couldn't follow what you were saying. As a former mentor once told me, every word should carry freight. So, if it's not necessary, delete it.

Natasha: Well, I guess I could delete my jobs before law school. I left in the job at the accounting firm because I thought perhaps that experience could be helpful.

Trish: While you're at it, I would eliminate your personal interests and hobbies. It's nice that you're well-rounded, but I don't think our attorneys much care about that.

Natasha: Really?

Trish: Yes, really. And your political experience, which seems interesting, could be off-putting. Bear in mind, most of the attorneys in our corporate group are of the Republican persuasion, and many are donors to like-minded politicians and causes.

My advice might be different if you didn't have the credentials and were on a nontraditional path to Biglaw. In that case, it may be strategically wise to include political type work on the theory that it's more likely to interest a person with a policy background than it is to put you out of the running for being on the wrong "side." I know that some partners, especially regulatory lawyers and policy wonks, enjoy seeing political work for mainstream organizations on either side of the aisle. Of course there is clearly downside risk here, but for a person who needs to catch a break before graduation, it might be a risk worth taking in order to stand out. But that is not you.

Natasha: Well, not yet anyway. I guess I'm not surprised to hear all of that.

Trish: Right. Also, your experience at the accounting firm might have been helpful, but I couldn't understand what you did. You need to explain what "accounting methods" are, and how your work would be relevant to our corporate clients.

Natasha: Well, with all due respect Trish, I think corporate lawyers do know about accounting methods.

Trish: Perhaps, but in its current form, there's a good chance your resume will never be seen by a lawyer, at least not a big firm lawyer.

Natasha: Ouch.

Trish: Sorry.

Natasha: It's okay. Accounting methods are rules under which companies keep their financial records and prepare their financial reports.

Trish: Ah. So, are there special methods for oil and gas companies? I ask because our headquarters are in Houston, and most of our clients are from that industry.

Natasha: Actually, yes there are. I advised a handful of oil and gas clients on the two approaches in that industry referred to as successful efforts accounting and full cost accounting. There are many differences between the two approaches, but the main one is that in the first method, the costs for unsuccessful exploration—where the company does not find oil or gas—is expensed, and the expensing of the item shows up on the income statement. In the second method, the cost is capitalized and does not show up on the income statement.

Trish: Too much detail already, and you lost me. I am no expert, but can you think of ways your understanding of accounting could bring value to our corporate clients?

Natasha: Sorry, I do tend to get lost in the details. Absolutely. I think understanding how financial statements relate to each other and being able to see and understand the financial and tax effects of legal transactions would be valuable in a transactional practice, including doing due diligence and negotiating or structuring deals.

Trish: So, your expertise would translate to more effective negotiating and papering of various deals?

Natasha: Wow, how did you do that?

Trish: This isn't my first rodeo.

Natasha: I guess not. Yes, to answer your question. That's essentially what I am saying.

Trish: Well, a couple of thoughts from a layman. You may want to consider putting that thought front and center in a cover letter.

Natasha: Ah. Good idea!

Trish: That reminds me. I came across a quote recently that might be helpful to you. (Trish spends a few moments sorting through papers on her desk.) Okay, found it. Thanks for your patience. The quote is — "The resume focuses on you and the past. The cover letter focuses on the employer and the future. Tell the hiring professional what you can do to benefit the organization in the future." The quote is from a book called *Cover Letters for Dummies*. Have you read it? It's by Joyce Lain Kennedy.

Again, this shows you should prepare your resume from the perspective of the person reading it, not the person writing it. I think this adjustment of perspective will also help you immensely once you work at the law firm.

Natasha: That makes sense. But two questions come to mind. How exactly do I do that? And how does one learn the perspective of the person reading the resume?

Trish: Good questions. Let's see if I can address both at the same time. The person reading your resume has to relate what you've done to what he or she is looking for. I would make it easy for him or her in two ways. First, if you have a law firm in mind, find out its bread-and-butter clients and their challenges and goals. This is what I mean when I talk about the employer's perspective. Tailor your work experience descriptions to show you're equipped to handle those challenges and obtain the results for which the clients are looking. Second, make the point clear by adding a cover letter and stating it there.

Natasha: Okay. Another question comes to mind. How much detail should I put on the resume? You said I had too much in certain areas, but I didn't explain enough in others.

Trish: Fair question. For that, you may want to get advice from lawyers working at your dream firm. But, let's look at the generic description you wrote— *Analytical professional offering extensive experience as a tax accountant in support of a public accounting firm. Expertise in general accounting, financial reporting (including accounting methods), and related income tax preparation issues.*

Those fancy words don't say much, in my humble opinion. Remember, you have your previous position and the company name in your heading, so cut to the chase and make it relevant to the law firm's clients, namely top oil and gas companies. My suggestion would be something along these lines—*Practice included advising Forbes 500 clients in the oil and gas industry on financial reporting, including accounting methods and related income tax treatment issues.*

Short and sweet. Also, as discussed, I would add a short cover letter. Perhaps something like—"I understand the corporate group represents oil and gas companies on M&A and other transactions. I think my knowledge of the accounting and tax effects and specifically my expertise in the oil and gas industry will be helpful to clients in investigating, negotiating, and structuring its transactions and helping them achieve desired goals. I look forward to learning more about your practice and about how I can potentially contribute."

Note that the benefit of talking to real live corporate lawyers at your dream firm is that they may be able to share some of the challenges and goals of their clients. This piece is currently missing from the cover letter. Instead of the generic "desired goals," consider how much more powerful it would be to mention specific challenges and objectives in the letter.

Natasha: Wow, Trish. This has been enormously helpful.

Trish: No problem. I am glad. I'll tell you what, I will check with one of our corporate guys and ask him if he would chat with you when he has time. He can fill in the missing pieces and perhaps keep you in mind if one of our summer associates doesn't work out.

Natasha: That would be awesome. Thank you, Trish. I appreciate all the time you spent.

Trish: My pleasure.

The meeting between Natasha and Trish illustrates the key for success when crafting resumes. Natasha, like most law students, wrote her resume from her perspective rather than the reader's. As Trish advised, Natasha is likely to have better luck once she switches her orientation, which involves considering how her experience can help her employers, and addressing their challenges and goals. Trish also recommended the use of a cover letter to highlight the benefits she can offer a potential employer. That approach is exactly what Freddy used in the case study below.

Case Study: Freddy's Cover Letter

A 3L at a third-tier law school, Freddy had barely made the top third of his class. He had no job prospects, but he was interested in litigation.

Freddy's law school posted a position with a small commercial litigation firm whose founders were alumni of his law school. The posting was general and did not offer much information:

> Looking for new associate interested in commercial and employment litigation matters before federal and state courts. Cases involve a wide variety of substantive issues, including corporate governance and control, breach of contract, and commercial and residential landlord-tenant disputes. Experience and strong academic credentials required.

Freddy felt he did not have "strong academic credentials." He thought he could go with the experience angle, but this would be tough because his only legal job had been as a research assistant for the professor who taught his Civil Procedure course.

Not wishing to waste his time or the firm's, Freddy tried to obtain more information from his law school career office. When this approach was unsuccessful, he tried to call the hiring partner, Mr.

Peterson, who was also an alumnus of his law school. Here is a transcript of that call.

> **Freddy:** Hi, I'm Freddy Pagani. I'm thinking of applying to become a new associate at your firm. Before I apply, I thought I'd find out directly what the firm's looking for. Would it be possible for me to have a brief meeting, five minutes or less, with your boss, Mr. Peterson? I would like to find out what the firm's ideal candidate would look like.
>
> **Mr. Peterson's secretary:** Hello, Mr. Pagani. Mr. Peterson is very busy and doesn't have time to talk to every applicant. My advice is to send your resume and see what happens.
>
> **Freddy:** I appreciate that, but I think I can be helpful. If I could find out exactly what experience the firm is looking for, I can include my relevant experience in the application. Also, I can give this information to my law school's career office. Then you'll get the most relevant and qualified students applying. Could I please leave my name, number, and e-mail address for Mr. Peterson? If he doesn't get back to me, I'll understand. Are you comfortable with that?
>
> **Mr. Peterson's secretary:** Sure. Better yet, just e-mail me your information and exactly what you told me and I will forward it to Mr. Peterson.
>
> **Freddy:** Thank you for your help and time. Will do.

Freddy wrote the e-mail and received a forwarded response from Mr. Peterson's secretary the next day. In the brief e-mail, Mr. Peterson wrote:

The firm has a large volume of landlord-tenant cases, representing the landlord in the three local jurisdictions, and needs someone familiar with the law and the courts and who is capable of handling these cases from the start. The perfect candidate is a self-starter, can handle heavy responsibility, including writing with little supervision, and has a good natured and pleasant demeanor, even when under pressure.

As it turned out, Freddy had relevant experience. Here is what he wrote:

Dear Mr. Peterson:

I am writing in response to your firm's posting at the law school for a commercial litigation associate. I understand that you are looking for someone with experience in landlord-tenant law and prefer a candidate who can hit the ground running and handle these matters right away.

I am that person. My family has been in the rental real estate business for about 20 years, and I own rental real estate units in the three local jurisdictions. In order to run a profitable side business and protect my investment, I have had to become familiar with the state laws in each of these places. This took a bit of time, but I was eager to get up to speed and figured that I could save some costs by learning the law myself. Importantly, I've obtained successful results in dealing with a variety of legal issues concerning rent, deposits, repairs, evictions, property damages, and accidents on the properties, as well as other issues. In most of these cases, I generally serve as my own counsel and have benefited from my coursework at law school, where I have covered negotiation, settlement, and alternative dispute resolution.

I would apply the same enthusiasm and diligence to your clients' cases as I do my own. Frankly, I enjoy the work, and I think my successful experiences and relevant coursework would be beneficial to your clients.

Thank you for your consideration. I look forward to meeting with you and learning more about your firm and its clients.

Sincerely,

Freddy Pagani

♦ ♦ ♦

Freddy got the interview and landed his dream job. Mr. Peterson told Freddy that the cover letter had convinced him and that he didn't even look at the resume. Freddy was clear and concise in his letter, showing that he could write. Mr. Peterson said to him: "You did your homework, so you knew what the heck it is we do around here, and what we needed. Instead of bragging how great you are, you explained exactly how your experience and coursework could benefit the firm and its clients. Very powerful."

Can you replicate Freddy's success? Absolutely. Note that Freddy called the firm first because he understood the value of thinking like the employer. He explained the specific skills he brought that were required for the position and the experiences he had that backed up his ability to work in landlord–tenant law. He drew attention to his achievements in areas that would benefit the firm. To this impressive list, he added some of his relevant cognitive abilities, such as writing and negotiating. He closed with some attractive habits, such as enthusiasm and diligence.

Freddy was successful because he spent time thinking about what the firm would care about and created a cover letter around these items. That approach was enough to land the job. In the event that it wasn't, the hiring partner could have reviewed Freddy's resume and verified the points he made in his cover letter.

Just as Freddy succeeded by focusing on what the employer thinks about and needs, Claire nailed her call back interviews with an employer-oriented 30-second commercial.

Case Study: Claire's 30-Second Commercial

Although Claire graduated with excellent grades from a top 20 law school, she was still looking for a job. Uncertainty about her choice of legal career had led Claire to skip the fall interviewing program. She had attended meetings in the career office many times with little success. Claire's luck changed two months after graduation, when she received a call from the head of the career office, Lily.

Lily had a close relationship with an alumnus who was a partner in a big firm. She was calling to give Claire the opportunity to interview over the phone as a first-year associate in the firm's tax department. Lily advised Claire to prepare for the phone interview by putting together a 30-second commercial. The purpose of the commercial was to translate Claire's general legal experience and education into something that the firm would find helpful. Here is a partial transcript of the conversation between Lily and Claire.

>**Claire:** I am not sure where to start. I've no experience with 30-second commercials, and I don't think my small amount of tax experience will help the firm.
>**Lily:** Wait, you have some tax experience?
>**Claire:** Yes. When I was in law school, I spent a year working in the general counsel's office at the Museum

of Art. While I was there, we were overwhelmed with questions from the IRS. The IRS wanted to know which of the museum's activities were consistent with its exempt status and which ones triggered unrelated business income tax. We met with the IRS to explain the nature of the museum's activities and demonstrate compliance with the rules. My boss was very adept at explaining it all.

Lily: That's great, Claire. My understanding is that the firm helps a lot of health care clients in dealings with the IRS concerning their tax-exempt status. As they are both tax-exempt entities, it seems that museums may have similar tax issues as health care non-profits. Right?

Claire: Yes, they might.

Lily: Okay. What was the upshot of those meetings you had with the IRS?

Claire: Well, the cases weren't resolved while I was there, but we were in the process of answering the IRS inquiries. My boss hoped that our follow-up written responses would resolve most or all of the open matters.

Lily: Good. So, my advice is that you use your experience with the museum to show how you could address similar challenges of the firm's clients in dealing with the Internal Revenue Code rules and regulations governing tax-exempt organizations. Also, since you haven't shown any interest in tax before, it might be helpful to explain what you like about it. Otherwise, they might think you only want to work in tax law because there's a job available.

Claire: That all makes sense.

Lily: Great, Claire. If you put yourself in the firm's shoes and consider who you would hire, I think you'll do well.

Claire: Okay, thanks, Lily. I'll give it a shot. May I e-mail you my 30-second commercial once it's finished?

Lily: Please do. I'll get back to you with my thoughts.

Here is the text of the 30-second commercial Claire sent to Lily:

I don't have deep experience in any area of the law as all my work experience was very general in nature. However, I have some experience in tax and thought the work was pretty interesting. I like the idea that tax is so woven into every decision a business makes because this means there is potential for a lot of variety in the work. Tax is complex and intricate. It appeals to me because I like puzzles.

I have no experience with health care clients, but I do have some experience with museums, and to some extent, I believe the principles are the same. For example, I worked for a short time at the general counsel's office dealing with questions from the IRS concerning whether some of the museum's activities were consistent with its exempt status and whether some of its activities triggered unrelated business income tax.

Lily gave Claire her feedback on the commercial. Here is the text of the commercial after Claire incorporated Lily's comments:

To assist your health care clients, I would draw upon my experience working on thorny tax issues facing a tax-exempt museum.

I worked in the general counsel's office at the Museum of Art, and the office was overwhelmed with questions from the IRS concerning whether some of the museum's activities were consistent with its exempt status and whether some of its activities triggered unrelated business income tax.

During my tenure, our legal team was in the process of providing the IRS the detail needed in easy, digestible (written and oral) formats to understand the operations of the museum and support the tax positions taken. I have since followed up with my former colleagues and learned that, notwithstanding the barrage of inquiries received and the extensive education required to get the IRS up to speed on the museum's activities, the IRS has indeed closed 80 percent of the open matters on which I worked. My colleagues credited my relatability, diligence, and writing skills as crucial to our successful effort. I hope to have the opportunity to bring these skills to your firm and its health care clients.

Lily stressed that Claire didn't have to say every line of the commercial to be effective. In fact, just the process of thinking about, preparing, and revising it would be very good preparation for the interview.

Claire reported back to Lily that her interview went well because she focused on the specifics of how her experience could be helpful. One of the interviewer's first questions was "How can you help our clients?"— a softball given Claire's preparation. Claire told Lily that the exercise of crafting her commercial forced her to consider that it was the IRS's lack of understanding of the activities of the museum that, in large part, triggered its audits. This exercise gave Claire clarity about what skills and activities were needed to solve the challenge.

It turned out the firm's hospitals faced the same problem. The IRS needed facts to show that they were compliant with Internal Revenue Code. The hospitals' focus on IRS matters was taking the firm's attention away from other pressing legal matters. Thus, Claire's experience was directly relevant. She understood the obstacles and had experience overcoming them. As of this writing, Claire has received a call back for a second interview from the firm.

Takeaways

The key to Natasha's resume, Freddy's cover letter, and Claire's 30-second commercial was to be clear on what each of them were bringing to the table from their dream employer's perspective. These examples show that when looking for a job, it is not enough for you to understand your assets. You need to communicate that you have the specific skills, experience, results, and habits your dream employer needs.

◆ ◆ ◆

Samples of effective resumes and cover letters can be downloaded at www.LegalJob.com/Resources.

CHAPTER 5

Become an Expert on the Employer

"To succeed in business, you need to be original, but you also need to understand what your customers want." —Richard Branson

The experiences of Natasha, Freddy, and Claire in Chapter Four show how important it is to see things from an employer's perspective when looking for a job. It is not enough to think like an employer, however. To succeed, job candidates must become experts on them.

To become an expert on an employer and utilize this knowledge when finding a job, you need to follow three steps: First, obtain a clear understanding of the results the employer is seeking and the resources it needs to attain those results. Second, demonstrate this deep, clear, and specific understanding. Third, articulate why hiring you is the best way to get the employer the results it wants. This chapter provides strategies for executing each of these steps. These strategies will work regardless of the size and type of business—law firm, corporation, government agency, etc.—or the nature of the work.

Why Is It Important to Become an Expert on the Employer?

If an employer feels that a prospective employee really understands its mission, culture, frustrations, challenges, and goals, it is more likely to hire and retain that person. This is also true of clients, who will be more likely to seek your services if you demonstrate a deep understanding of their professional and personal challenges, aspirations, and needs. Therefore, honing this skill will serve you in getting the job and excelling in the legal profession.

If you go into the interview blind, you leave your prospects of getting the job to circumstance and other factors outside your control.

The solution outlined below involves doing most of the hard work before the interview. This approach gives you more control of the situation. It may be unconventional, but it works.

Step One: Dig Deep to Understand the Firm and Its Clients

To obtain a deeper understanding of your potential employer, you need to know the types of major clients it serves (inside and outside of the practice area for which you are interviewing), the business and legal challenges faced by its clients, the strategies it adopts, and the ideal outcomes of its clients. In addition, you should understand what the firm is looking for in terms of personnel and clients, and its future objectives. For big law firms, you should also set out to understand the general pressures and expectations that come in that setting. For this purpose, talk with lawyers who aren't actively recruiting you and can be completely candid. So rely on family, friends, and even friends of friends for these conversations. Of course there are differences between firms, but there are also a lot of similarities regarding the dynamics and atmosphere. In those conversations, one can also learn differences between the various types of practices as well.

Use the following methods to obtain information on a potential employer:

First, you can research information online, including a career guide such as *Chambers Associate* (online at www.chambers-associate.com/home), which provides detailed information on the life of associates at the top law firms. The Chambers information—on the day-to-day work, the lifestyle, and the training opportunities—is particularly helpful because it is taken from interviews with associates, firm chairs, managing partners, and hiring partners. Not all law firms are covered in the guide, however, especially smaller firms.

Second, e-mail one of the employer's junior associates and ask if you could have 10-15 minutes of his or her time. Explain that you wish to get up to speed to make sure that you are the right fit for the firm. What is the worst that can happen? He or she says "no"? Or doesn't respond?

Third, ask your career development office or professors for the contact information of any alumni who are past or present employees at the firm. All you need is one contact who is willing to provide you with more information than you would have if you were limited to the internet and the firm's website.

Step Two: Demonstrate that You Understand the Firm

Next, you need to be able to demonstrate this knowledge of the firm and its clients. You should show this understanding in your interview and other communications, including your cover letter, resume, and 30-second commercial. While you articulate this understanding, you should seek feedback on whether you are correct and be open to deepening your knowledge with even more information. This requires you to project both confidence and humility.

Step Three: Explain How You Can Help the Employer Achieve Its Objectives

Describe how your background, experience, and education position you to help solve the clients' legal challenges and obtain the ideal outcomes desired. You should not focus on explaining your past decisions and outlining your future goals and interests. And, you should definitely not attempt to present yourself as something you're not. Instead, you need to demonstrate how your credentials will translate to strong contributions for the firm.

Case Study: Corey and His Less-Than-Perfect Interview

Corey was a 3L in the top 10 percent at a top 30 law school. As a 2L, Corey had taken and excelled in several classes that interested him, including bankruptcy, commercial credit, secured financing, negotiations, and corporate finance. Corey did particularly well in bankruptcy, earning the highest grade in the class. Nonetheless, he was unfocused and somewhat lazy when it came to career planning and skipped the fall interviewing program.

Corey served as a research assistant for his bankruptcy professor, Jayne. When he mentioned to her that he had not yet secured employment, Jayne asked whether he would be interested in working in a bankruptcy practice at a top law firm. Given his success in Jayne's class and other related classes, Corey was very interested. Through Jayne's friend, who was a partner and bankruptcy practice leader at the law firm, Corey got an interview.

Before the interview, Corey learned from his professor that much of the firm's practice involved representing debtors in Chapter 11 actions. Jayne also mentioned that her friend worked long hours. Aside from this brief conversation about the firm with Jayne, and ten minutes spent perusing the firm's website, Corey did no preparation for the interview.

Although the interview with Karl, the firm's partner, seemed short, Corey thought it went well. So, he was surprised when he wasn't asked back to meet with the other attorneys in the group.

After some small talk about sports and Karl's short description of the firm's makeup and office, the interview went at follows:

> **Karl:** Jayne suggested you might be able to help our firm. Tell me, why are you interested in working here?
> **Corey:** Jayne thought your firm and its bankruptcy practice would be a good fit because of my strong performance in her class and the related coursework.

Also, it sounds like there's some variety in the practice, including opportunities to be in court and get transactional experience negotiating deals throughout the bankruptcy process.

Karl: There is variety, both in terms of our clients and what we do for them. We work with distressed companies, debtors, trustees, secured and unsecured creditors, defendants in insolvency-related litigation, and purchasers of distressed assets. There is a "jack-of-all-trades" aspect to the practice. You might find yourself negotiating with creditors to keep a business going, creating employee retention packages, or going to court and litigating issues. So, you'll get exposure to both—the Perry Mason side in the courtroom and the deal-making side in the conference room.

Corey: Well, I think I can help in both areas. I have some "hands-on" litigation experience and exposure. I took part in a legal clinic, helping low-income clients deal with housing, domestic violence, and employment civil controversies. I think I was successful because I was a quick study, along with having persuasive abilities and strong writing skills. I also did well in my negotiations course. Would it be helpful to elaborate on some of my litigation achievements?

Karl: Not now, thanks. Tell me Corey, is there anything that concerns you about working at this firm or in the bankruptcy field?

Corey: Well, it sounds like the hours are long, which is okay. Are they predictable, though? I ask because, in the winter, I like to spend my weekends skiing whenever possible.

Karl: Unfortunately, the hours are often unpredictable, and nights and weekends are often lost when cases are in court.

Corey: Okay, well, that's understandable. Tell me, what type of training program do you have for new associates? Also, do you have a mentoring program?

Karl: Yes, we have a vibrant mentoring program. To get into our training, I think it would first be helpful if I tell you about a day in the life of a typical associate. Would you be open to hearing about it?

Corey: Sure.

The interview went on for another 15 minutes. When it ended, Corey and Karl exchanged pleasantries, and Karl told him the firm would be in touch in the next couple of weeks.

Here is a transcript of a subsequent conversation between Corey and Jayne.

Corey: Hi, Professor. I received a rejection letter from the firm, and I can't understand why. I thought the interview went well, and you said they were impressed with my academic credentials. Do you know what happened?

Jayne: I do. Did you follow up with Karl to ask him?

Corey: No. I just sent him an e-mail thanking him for meeting with me.

Jayne: E-mail, huh? I still prefer to get handwritten thank-you notes. It takes a little more time, but people appreciate the effort.

Corey: It seems like a lot of work for something that doesn't matter much.

Jayne: Well, it couldn't hurt, and it might help. Anyway, do you want me to tell you what Karl shared with me?

Corey: Please.

Jayne: He said that you made the interview about you. He thought you were more interested in what the firm could do to enhance your experience rather than what your experience could do to benefit the firm.

Corey: Huh? Why did he say that? What should I have done differently?

Jayne: I sense, from Karl's comments, that you weren't completely focused on how you could be of service to the firm and help it to succeed. Fair?

Corey: I thought the key to crushing the interview was to sell oneself, so I tried to do that by referencing my credentials and experience.

Jayne: You're partially correct. The objective is to look at your interview through the firm's eyes. Sure, you have the credentials. That is why I arranged the connection. But are any of your credentials relevant to helping the firm achieve its goals?

Corey: I see. Darn. Perhaps I should have spent more time prepping.

Jayne: Perhaps. So, how would your experience at the clinic or as my research assistant help the firm to get what it wants or needs? What does the firm want or need? What are the biggest challenges facing it and its clients?

Corey: I have no idea.

Jayne: I don't know either. But you could have connected with one of the junior associates before the interview to find out.

Corey: People do that? Get that type of intel ahead of time?

Jayne: Why not?

Corey: I had no idea.

Jayne: Another technique you can try in the future is to ask the interviewer these types of questions.

Corey: I'm afraid that would feel like I was hijacking the interview. How do I draw an interviewer out on those things?

Jayne: Good question. The idea is to make interviewers feel comfortable sharing. Treat them as if they were the center of your world. Hang onto their every word. Ask relevant, thought-provoking questions and follow-up questions. Reiterate what they say to confirm your understanding. In the future, you will need the same skills when dealing with clients.

Corey: I suppose I could work on my listening skills.

Jayne: Yes. But it's not just about listening. You need to understand the firm's challenges before you can determine whether and how you can help. The more you know about the firm, the easier it will be for you to articulate how you can help.

Corey: Interesting. All this time, I figured the firm's challenge is getting enough competent folks to do the legal work.

Jayne: At that firm, I am not sure they have too much trouble finding qualified employees. Given the state of the legal industry, it's more likely that they are focused on dealing with the challenges of greater pricing competition, practice efficiency, and commoditization of legal work. If I recall correctly, don't you have some computer background?

Corey: Yep. I have some computer programming skills and trade domain names from time to time.

Jayne: Okay, good. Then keep in mind that your technology experience or social media prowess might be helpful. You could use a computer to keep track of the procedural posture of the various cases.

Corey: Well, I had that experience on my resume, so he could have asked about it.

Jayne: That assumes a lot. Do we know whether he read your resume?

Corey: Fair point. Man, I am sorry that I wasted such a great opportunity. So, is selling oneself an outdated idea?

Jayne: It's not selling yourself that's outdated. It's your approach to selling yourself. The key is to switch the focus to the person you are trying to serve.

Corey: Professor, thanks for spending so much time with me on this and connecting me to the firm, even though I blew it. I think I understand what I need to do next time.

Jayne: My pleasure, Corey. And I'll keep my ears open for other opportunities.

Corey: Cool. Thanks.

Corey got a crash course from Jayne about both the importance of switching one's orientation away from self and becoming an expert on the firm. Krista, discussed next, demonstrates the benefit of applying these principles.

Case Study: Krista Hits Her Interview Out of the Park

Krista was a 3L in the top 20 percent of her law school class. In her first year, Krista had achieved mediocre grades and was unsuccessful in the fall interviewing program. Nonetheless, she clawed her way back to the top in her second and third year by taking and excelling in all tax and business type classes. Krista was prompted to take these classes near the end of her first year, after attending a tax career panel at her law school. Krista had listened closely when one of the panelists, a partner at a top law firm, had emphasized the importance of focusing and picking a major. Krista had heeded the panelist's advice, and just one month before graduating, she had lined up an interview to practice tax litigation with a big law firm.

Before the interview, the folks in the career development office advised Krista to learn as many details as she could about the firm, its tax practice, and the nature of the work. One of her law school classmates, Megan, was in the labor and employment group of the firm's first year associate class. Krista took Megan out to lunch to enlist her help. Below is a transcript of their conversation:

> **Krista:** Hey Meg, could you help me prepare for my interview by finding out some things about the tax group? I think you mentioned that you were friends with one of the labor associates.
>
> **Megan:** Yes, Elle is her name. Sure. It would be awesome to work at the same firm! What do you need to know?
>
> **Krista:** Here, I have a list. (Krista presents the detailed list).
>
> **Megan:** Wow, Krista. This is intense. I didn't know any of these things when I interviewed. Are you overthinking this interview and trying too hard?
>
> **Krista:** Remember, you came through the regular fall interviewing program channel and are in the top 5 percent. There is probably not much you could have

said to derail your chances. We are graduating in one month, so I need to do whatever I can to improve my chances.

Here is Krista's list:

Things to Find Out about the Firm

1. What is the composition of the tax group? The website suggests there are no associates and six partners. Can that be right?
2. Does the firm want to grow its tax group? Does the firm want to grow overall?
3. What are the firm's main areas of focus?
4. Do the partners work collaboratively with associates providing them with a chance to grow?
5. What is the makeup of clients and their industries (inside and outside of the tax group)?
6. Why is the firm an excellent choice for young lawyers?
7. What types of legal matters are handled? Controversy versus transactional split?
8. What is the firm's mission statement?
9. What attributes does the firm look for in a new associate?
10. What type of prior experience is helpful to the firm and the tax group?

Megan worked hard to answer the items on Krista's list. She also received help from third-year associate, Elle, who was so impressed with the scope of the list that she discussed the answers over coffee with one of the tax partners. Krista felt very prepared going into her interview with the firm. Here is a transcript of part of the interview:

Roger: Would you be interested in learning about some of the controversy matters we are handling?

Krista: Yes, I would, and I appreciate you sharing.

Roger: One of the matters is in Tax Court, and it involves the characterization of whether certain foreign trading losses are capital or ordinary in nature. They were originally filed as capital losses, but as they total over $100 million, the client is having second thoughts and would prefer to deduct them immediately rather than over time.

Krista: Interesting. Are the facts agreed, so that it is just a legal interpretation, or are the facts at play?

Roger: Good question. It is a little of both. There are two different code sections that could apply. One results in capital treatment, and one results in ordinary. The question of which applies is mostly fact based.

Krista: I see. Does it require a lot of time spent going through trading and related documents, interpreting them, and figuring out what documents are missing?

Roger: Indeed, it does.

Krista: That sounds like an interesting case. I don't have experience with that area of the Code, but my experience at the tax boutique involved heavy document review. We had to look at every page of thousands of pages being submitted to the IRS agent. The aim was to ensure there was no smoking gun in the materials or, at least, to be able to explain anything that might be perceived as unhelpful to the taxpayer's case.

Roger: I know how that goes. How did you find that process?

Krista: It was tedious and time intensive, but I enjoyed knowing that our willingness to review the papers so carefully might give us an advantage. The work had significant ramifications for the client's case. And because the client was fee sensitive, we had to explain why the work took so many hours.

Roger: That is a great and unusual perspective.

Krista: Thank you. So, Roger, on that case, what would be most helpful to you and the client? I understand there are no associates in the group at present. Is that correct?

Roger: Sadly, that's right. We came over from another firm one year ago and didn't bring the associates. The firm brought us over because it is interested in growing its tax group. We plan to bring on associates, perhaps starting with you.

Krista: I would be very interested in contributing to your group as the first associate.

Roger: We need an associate to work on this case, someone who can spend hours examining these documents. This person should add value and raise strategic and factual considerations. The facts can be problematic, and the client doesn't always provide them in their entirety. Therefore, we need someone who is deeply curious.

Krista: I get it. And I would be glad to help. Can I ask a bit more about the case?

Roger: Sure.

Krista: Is trading the client's main business? Perhaps that's one of the factual questions that govern the tax treatment. How long was the trading going on and how does this case affect your client day to day? Is he or she anxious to get this resolved?

Roger: You ask thoughtful questions. The client is a medical surgeon, so this is really a hobby. However, given the time and money spent, we may be able to argue that it's similar to a side business. The client would like the case to be complete, but it's not affecting him financially, and it doesn't affect his medical practice.

Krista: I see. Fascinating.

Roger: Krista, what else can I tell you about our group or the firm?

Krista: Would you mind if I summarize my understanding about the tax group and its needs? I want to confirm what I believe you're looking for in an associate and suggest how I think I can help.

Roger: That sounds fine.

Krista: Thanks. Your clients include wealthy individuals, estates, and companies. Most of the work is in the tax controversy space, which includes both court and administrative proceedings, such as IRS audits and IRS appeals. Sometimes, your clients seek transactional help, but this work is less common. You could use an associate, or perhaps two, to pitch in wherever possible, specifically for intensive document review and to keep track of open matters for some of your more demanding individual clients. You need someone who understands that in certain contexts you may function as a business lawyer that specializes in tax. Is that close?

Roger: That's all correct. Nice job. Krista, you ask thoughtful questions and listen well. Now, what do you think is the most helpful thing you learned from your experience working at the tax boutique firm?

Krista: Thank you. Well, the partner I worked for was very effective, in large part because he understood the client's concerns. He held regular meetings with the client and its employees, and he was very relatable. Whenever he talked with the client, he provided the information in an easy to understand, digestible format. I hope I can emulate him as much as possible.

Roger: Those are great attributes and something we value as well. Krista, you give a great interview, and I think the tax group would be lucky to have you as its first associate. Could you come back and meet with my partners next week?

Krista: That would be great. Thank you, Roger.

Needless to say, Krista nailed her call-back interview and was offered a position in the firm.

Takeaways

Krista gave a polished and well-received interview. With her extensive questionnaire, she dug deep to understand the firm and its clients ahead of time. She followed that up in the interview with questions that confirmed her understanding of the tax group's personnel needs. Rather than selling herself by listing her accomplishments, Krista helped the firm answer the question of why it should consider hiring her, inserting her experience only when it was relevant to the discussion.

Krista also demonstrated that she was clear about the type of matters on which the group worked. While articulating this understanding, she also sought feedback on whether she was correct and seemed open to learning more. That flexibility showed a nice combination of confidence and humility.

Krista clearly demonstrated how she could be helpful in solving the clients' legal challenges and obtaining the ideal outcomes desired. Unlike Corey, she did not focus on her own achievements, ambitions, and credentials, but on how she could help the firm to deal with its clients' problems and accomplish its clients' goals.

♦ ♦ ♦

A checklist to help you stay on track as you become an expert on a specific employer and a description of the primary attributes legal employers look for in a candidate can be downloaded at www.LegalJob.com/Resources.

CHAPTER 6

Focus on the Plan, Not the Outcome

"Without strategy, execution is aimless. Without execution, strategy is useless."—Morris Chang

As a stressed-out job seeker, you probably find it difficult to concentrate on your plan rather than the interesting and highly paid job you want when you graduate. After all, to pay off your monster loans, you need to secure and hold down that job.

You will not achieve better, faster results with anxiety and impatience, however. Quite the opposite. Has frenetic thinking ever helped you to solve problems? If you set aside your angst and follow the process outlined in this book, you can take some comfort in knowing that the approach offered here will give you a leg up amongst your peers, increasing your chances of securing the perfect job. As with anything else in life, this process may not follow a linear, sequential path. Things do not always happen according to plan.

This chapter is designed to help you prepare for the unexpected and ambiguous twists and turns of the job searching process. It provides advice on implementing a long view strategy that should help keep you sane and bring your actions into alignment with your goals.

Beware of Two "Saboteurs"

If you are anything like me (and most lawyers I know), you occasionally suffer from two ailments that, if left unchecked, will inhibit your ability to make progress on each of the steps discussed in this book and ultimately prevent you from landing your ideal job.

The first is procrastination—the inability to begin projects.

The second is perfectionism—the tendency to never be finished with projects.

I have suffered from both from time to time. Sometimes I relapse and need a gentle (and occasionally not so gentle) reminder from a colleague, my wife, or my business coach to help get me unstuck. You need to be vigilant and crush these saboteurs when recognized. If I hadn't, I would never have landed a job at a big firm, made partner, published my first book or this book, or launched my coaching practice.

To tackle procrastination, it is helpful (if not mandatory) to set a start date for a project and a fixed deadline for completing the various tasks within each step. The deadline should be realistic, not too aggressive, but absolute. Pair your deadline with a way to hold yourself accountable for getting it done. Enlist the help of a friend, relative, or coach to check in with you to confirm your progress at key points along the way and to confirm you are finished by your target date.

To confront perfectionism, recognize that pursuing it is like pursuing the horizon. It will always be in your sights, but never be within your grasp. When performing any task related to finding a job, take off your lawyer hat. Don't overthink the task. You don't have to consider every possible context or contingency. Not every decision requires a comprehensive mental debate. Not every writing requires perfect prose or the air-tight language of a contract. Focus on making forward progress and getting the task completed rather than achieving perfection.

Stay Committed to Your Plan

This advice sounds obvious, doesn't it? Well, it isn't obvious for many law students. The job searching process can be difficult and may be filled with many setbacks. Law school doesn't train you to deal with the numerous obstacles that arise when searching for a job. Faced with negative results, many law students give up too soon, believing that their strategy will fail. Unlike many of these students, you have a proven plan, and you are committed to seeing it through. You will have negative thoughts. You may be concerned that you are not achieving results quickly enough, that you are not good enough for the jobs you are seeking, or that your strategy won't work. The path to success simply requires that you stay committed to the plan, however. Do whatever it takes to keep moving forward.

One activity that law students find particularly helpful is to keep a weekly journal to document their adherence to the process, regardless of the results. The activity of recording their work on or toward any of the six steps helps them feel committed to themselves and seeing the plan through. Many students find that after a month of writing journal entries, they feel unstoppable. When they encounter roadblocks (real and imagined), they think of ways around or over them. Instead of stopping when they feel uncomfortable or overwhelmed, they continue implementing the plan. Eventually, the roadblocks disappear because they no longer serve a purpose.

Question Everything You Think

If your mind works anything like mine did when I was looking for my first legal job, it will generate tons of limiting thoughts that are not helpful and, in many cases, not even true. It is best to question these thoughts when they arise, so they don't interfere with your plan. Two common misconceptions relate to timing and outcome.

<u>Timing</u>

You may think you need to line up your job by a certain date, perhaps by January of your third year in law school or at least, before graduation. However, I secured a job within two months of graduation. Many of my coaching clients had the same experience. A sizeable handful of them obtained their desired jobs months after graduation. So, do not get hung up on timing. Stay committed to the plan.

Outcome

Rejections are harsh. You may be tempted to take away from rejections that you will never be good enough. That is not true. In fact, if you learn from rejections, making changes and improvements where necessary, they can turn you into an even stronger candidate. Every rejection is an opportunity for you to seek honest and helpful feedback. With proper feedback, you can change or improve such factors as grade point average in relevant law courses, the number of relevant courses taken in a practice area, the amount of substantive legal experience in the relevant area, and interview demeanor. If you reapply for a position, having made these changes, the employer may reconsider or lock you in for a future opportunity.

Case Study: Stanley

Stanley had a plan. He wanted to become a litigator at a big city law firm. He also had an opportunity. Bert, an old friend of his father, was an executive at a national title insurance company. Bert arranged for Stanley to work as an intern in the legal department of the firm during his first law school summer. Stanley planned to complement that experience with relevant classes in the litigation area.

Stanley got mediocre grades in his first year, however. Believing this to be a true reflection of his limitations, he fell into a rut. He wondered whether he was cut out to be a firm litigator, or even a lawyer at all.

Negative thoughts plagued Stanley: "Do I need to start networking like crazy? But how do I network, and who will want to help me after my dismal performance? Should I even waste my time with the fall interviewing program? The firms that participate only look at first year grades. Should I lower my expectations? Maybe I should consider a job in a smaller city or town."

Stanley let his thoughts have tremendous power over him. As a result, he wasn't excited about his internship. He thought there might be no point showing up, let alone exerting much effort in the job.

Stanley called his dad, Trevor, and told him that he was considering flaking out on the internship and dropping out of law school. Trevor, who had paid half of Stanley's tuition bills, was not too pleased to hear that his investment might be wasted. He was also incensed that Stanley would even think about passing up the internship opportunity that Bert had worked hard to secure. Trevor insisted that Stanley meet with Bert to gain his perspective.

Here is an excerpt of Stanley's conversation with Bert.

> **Stanley:** I am just trying to be realistic. Given my poor performance, my odds of getting an associate position at a top law firm are probably zero. So, I think I need a contingency plan. Maybe, I'm not meant to be a lawyer. I'm obviously not very good at thinking or writing like one.
>
> **Bert:** Well, I didn't go to law school, so I don't have first-hand knowledge. However, I got some insight on your situation from Blair, who manages our legal division.
>
> **Stanley:** Thank you for doing that. I guess my dad gave you the heads up?
>
> **Bert:** Yes, he did. Blair had a couple of nuggets I thought might be helpful. He wondered why you were thinking about a contingency plan, rather than focusing on getting good grades over the next two years.

Stanley: Well, I was hoping for a starting salary of $180,000. So, I was thinking that my first year grades might make that impossible. If I graduate in the bottom 10 percent, will I have any shot at those jobs?

Bert: I don't know, but if it helps, Blair said there is no correlation between being a good test-taker and being a good lawyer. That said, he suggested you could make your situation stronger if you took more relevant courses over the next two years and excelled in them.

Stanley: Did he mention the courses that might be helpful for a career in litigation?

Bert: Yes, several. I wrote them down for you. If you are interested in financial services litigation, which is what we do here, he advised you to take courses dealing with disputes about adverse possession, boundary line, encroachment, priority, mechanics liens, the Real Estate Settlement Procedures Act, and the Truth in Lending Act claims.

Stanley: Thanks. That's a helpful list. Bert, does your legal department hire people straight out of law school?

Bert: Unfortunately, no. We hire from law firms. You would need to have worked at one for about five years.

Stanley: Okay. So, this is my biggest concern. How do I convince a firm to hire me with my grades?

Bert: Well Stanley, I can give you some direct advice here. You don't have to convince anyone to do anything.

Stanley: I don't?

Bert: No. It's just like dealing with clients. You can't convince them to do something, but you can help them discover why it's in their best interest to take a particular course of action. In the case of potential employers, you want to demonstrate that you understand their challenges and their goals. You need to show that you, with your education and work experience, have the tools to help them face those challenges and achieve those goals.

Stanley: Interesting. How do I convey that?

Bert: According to Blair, you don't need to be too worried about the fall program. He advises you to research firms that litigate for clients in areas that interest you. Then, reach out to a junior associate at that firm, preferably someone with whom you have something in common, to request information on his or her firm and practice. This person might be an alumnus of your law school or undergraduate school. Ask the junior associate to describe what the firm looks for in an associate and to discuss the problems its lawyers typically solve for clients. Be sensitive about taking too much time, but if possible summarize what you have learned and ask the associate to confirm your understanding. Get the associate's recommendation on who best to send a cover letter and resume to for future reference, just in case the firm ever has an opening in the litigation group. In your cover letter, mention your discussion with the associate, demonstrate your knowledge of the firm, and describe how you believe you can help its clients. Even if you don't get an interview with that firm, your research may help you to get in the door at another firm with a similar practice and client base.

Stanley: Wow, this is really helpful, Bert. I'm starting to get excited about all this again. Maybe financial services litigation will be my thing?

Bert: Seems to have worked out well for Blair and his colleagues.

Stanley: I can't tell you how much I appreciate your advice, and Blair's.

Bert: You can show us by doing a bang-up job in your internship. Also, you probably don't need me to tell you this, but you should make sure to thank Blair directly.

Stanley: Absolutely. Thanks again, Bert.

Stanley went through with his internship with vigor. He contributed so much time, effort, and value to the company that he was asked to work there part-time during the school year. While working there, he got lots of hands-on experience, including opportunities to work with attorneys who were responsible for evaluating and responding to claims made under the company's various title insurance products, and participating in mediations, arbitrations, and trials.

As predicted, Stanley did not have much luck with the fall interviewing program. He managed to secure initial interviews with two firms that practiced financial services litigation, but these meetings were unsuccessful. Stanley followed up with the associates he met at these interviews, asking for five-minute calls to obtain feedback. In both calls, the associates said that although the interviewers had been impressed by Stanley's work experience, his grades and law school ranking were too low to merit a summer offer. Stanley did not despair. He had a solid plan and was committed to following it.

In his second and third year, Stanley took and excelled in many classes relevant to his area. These classes supplemented his hands-on training at the title firm. He also reached out to associates at firms that represented mortgage lenders and servicers, some of whom were very helpful. In January of his third year, Stanley had secured three interviews with law firms near his law school: two large law firms, and a small boutique firm.

Stanley was poised in his interviews and connected his relevant educational and work experience with the challenges facing the firms' clients. He received an offer from one of the large law firms and the boutique firm. Both firms reported that it was rare to have a candidate with such relevant academic and work experience and as tuned into their clients' challenges. In March of his third year, Stanley accepted an associate position at the large law firm, which represented mortgage lenders and servicers. Stanley's litigation practice was going to be focused on something he knew well: defending financial institutions from claims arising out of various consumer and commercial financial products.

◆ ◆ ◆

After a disappointing academic start, Stanley experienced an abundance of limiting thoughts. At first, he let these thoughts call the shots and even considered dropping out of law school. After consulting with a mentor and receiving solid career advice, Stanley committed to his plan and took action. If you experience a setback, you can do the same and get back on track.

Listen to Feedback and Course Correct Where Possible

Like most law students, you will probably have negative perceptions of your performance or abilities. Perhaps you think you could have handled certain things differently in your search for a legal job. Perhaps you believe that you lack certain credentials, including work experience or the right type of legal experience. You may have a less-than-stellar class standing or come from a law school with a low ranking. These negative perceptions are normal, but they might not be all that helpful in landing your dream legal job. Potential employers may have a completely different view of your abilities and deficiencies.

Instead of focusing on what you perceive as your faults and limitations, seek as much feedback as possible from potential employers. With their feedback and any modifications you are able to make as a result, you will become a stronger candidate.

The most opportune time to obtain this feedback is right after a rejection. The short and sweet form rejection letter does not have to be the end of the story. Before you begin your search for another opportunity, there is no harm in learning straight from the horse's mouth why the answer was "no."

The rejection may be based on something you can change or improve, such as a low grade point average, low grades in relevant law courses, an insufficient number of relevant courses taken in a practice area, no legal experience, no relevant legal experience, not enough responsibility in a previous legal job, no demonstrated commitment to a practice area, anxiety or nervousness during interview, or a failure to show enthusiasm. Perhaps it is something you cannot change, such as a personality quirk. Even if it turns out to be something you cannot change, knowing about your deficiency gives you the chance to compensate or to come up with a good reason why it doesn't matter.

In some cases, you may be inclined to ask for a chance to cure your deficiencies and reapply. There is nothing wrong with doing that. However, you are most likely to get helpful feedback if you are clear with the employer that you are not seeking to appeal the rejection but rather to improve your candidacy for other positions.

<u>Case Study: Thomas</u>

A 2L in the top 20 percent of his class at a top 10 law school, Thomas was interested in practicing corporate law at a top New York law firm. After participating in the fall interviewing program, he received several initial interviews from top firms. Thomas's first choice by far was a firm with a large global private equity funds practice. Thomas thought his brief interview with this firm went well. With his strong academic performance both at the undergraduate Ivy League school where he majored in finance and at his law school, he thought he had stellar credentials and expected to be called back. Consequently, Thomas was very surprised and disappointed to receive the following form rejection letter:

> Thank you for your interest. Although we were impressed with your qualifications, I regret to advise you that we are unable to consider your application at this time.
>
> We appreciate your interest and wish you every success in your professional endeavors.

"What? How could they reject me? And with a form letter," Thomas thought to himself. To add insult to injury, Thomas's friend and law school colleague, who had similar law school grades but had attended a state university as an undergraduate, received a call back from the firm. Here is an excerpt of a conversation between Thomas and his friend, Roland.

> **Thomas:** No offense, but it's crazy that you got the call back when my stats are superior. How could that happen?

Roland: Nice, buddy. Maybe they nixed you because of your winning personality.

Thomas: Yeah, right.

Roland: No, really. Perhaps you came off as too cocky.

Thomas: Well, I was respectful, but I am obviously confident with what I am bringing to the table.

Roland: Let me ask you something, Tom. Did you do any research on the firm, apart from a couple of minutes scanning their website?

Thomas: Not really. Is that necessary? I mean, how useful is the information online anyway?

Roland: Well, before my interview, I contacted an associate in the tax group, who also went to our law school, to get some information. I asked about the primary focus of the work the firm performed for its clients, some of the personalities of the tax partners, and the nature of the practice in general.

Thomas: That seems like a lot of work for an initial interview.

Roland: It didn't take long, and I think it was useful. I was able to refer to the call when I was answering questions about the tax group and the type of projects where I felt I could add the most value. It might have helped make up for what you call my crappy stats.

Thomas: Ha! Maybe so. I wish I could find out what went wrong in my interview.

Roland: You can.

Thomas: What do you mean?

Roland: Please tell me you still have the interviewers' cards?

Thomas: Um, I'm not sure. I think I remember their names.

Roland: Why don't you e-mail one or two of them? Ask them for five minutes of their time to get feedback on your interview.

Thomas: You can do that?

Roland: Sure, why not? The worst that can happen is you get no response. I'd make it clear that you're not appealing the rejection decision. Say you enjoyed your talk and would value any advice they might have for you going forward.

Thomas: Okay, thanks Rol. I'll try that.

Thomas received a response from Mitchell, one of the litigation associates with whom he interviewed. Mitchell agreed to a quick call. Here is an excerpt of their conversation.

Thomas: Hi, Mitchell. Thanks for taking the time to talk.

Mitchell: Sure, happy to.

Thomas: Mitchell, I was surprised that I didn't get a call back, given my credentials. Had you reached your associate class size, or was it something else?

Mitchell: Can I be completely honest with you, off the record?

Thomas: Yes, please.

Mitchell: Preston and I thought your interviewing style needed fine-tuning.

Thomas: Okay. How so?

Mitchell: You came off as a bit too self-assured and smug. Also, you didn't have much knowledge or interest in the firm, particularly outside the private equity fund practice.

Thomas: Okay. Perhaps that was nerves. Although, I didn't really scorch the earth when I was prepping for the interview because I didn't...

Mitchell: ...think you needed to, given your resume?

Thomas: I guess I was wrong.

Mitchell: You also seemed a bit excitable and not very comfortable chit-chatting. Added to that, your 1L summer job as a bartender didn't stack up against some of the other candidates, who got relevant legal experience during the break.

Thomas: Really? I didn't realize many 1Ls could get legal jobs.

Mitchell: Well, the two law students we called back from your law school did.

Thomas: Oh. Okay.

Mitchell: I think it's great that you were willing to hear this stuff. Very few folks follow up like you did.

Thomas: Well, I appreciate your candor. This call has been helpful to me, though hard to hear.

Mitchell: Oh, I'm happy to help. I don't know if you would have any interest in this, but one of my law school buddies works in the legal and compliance department of a financial service firm. I could put you in touch with him if you are interested.

Thomas: That would be awesome.

Mitchell: I'll shoot you my buddy's e-mail and let him know you'll be contacting him.

Thomas took a couple of days to digest Mitchell's feedback. He concluded that he probably did project a certain cockiness to mask his nerves. Furthermore, he had not done much to prepare for the interview, and he had no legal experience.

Before Thomas contacted Mitchell's friend at the financial service firm, he did some research. He learned that its compliance department hired summer associates to help attorneys with investigating claims, preparation of responses to certain requests, and legal and regulatory research. He thought that such a position could give him the type of legal experience that a law firm would value. Alternatively, and perhaps even more desirable, it might translate to a full-time position after law school.

Next, Thomas did some role-playing with his friend, Roland. From that experience, he came up with certain questions to ask Mitchell's friend, which would demonstrate his interest. These were:

What are some of the challenges you are facing? What are the outcomes you desire and the hurdles to achieving these outcomes? What kinds of people excel in the department? What personal qualities and prior experience do you look for when making hiring decisions?

It is unclear what will happen next for Thomas. However, his solicitation for feedback has clearly made him a stronger candidate, which may help him land a summer associate position in an area of interest. Thomas capitalized on the criticisms received by putting his preconceptions aside and altering his "me-oriented" approach.

Takeaways

After reading this chapter, you may think that you cannot necessarily recreate the success of Thomas and others. You may point out that Thomas was lucky because the employer agreed to provide detailed and helpful feedback. You may think that a successful father with quality contacts helped Stanley's case.

These are all reasonable thoughts.

However, law students who focus on the plan and not on less-than-desirable outcomes and feedback are able to create their own luck. This is because they position themselves mentally and physically to obtain the most benefit from an opportunity when it comes. Like all students, they get discouraged and overwhelmed, but their focus on their plan allows them to keep moving forward. When they are rejected, they maximize the opportunity by seeking feedback. Then, like Thomas, they implement the feedback and become even stronger candidates.

The techniques and strategies discussed in this chapter have helped many law students find a legal job. They will work for you as well.

◆ ◆ ◆

Tips on seeking post-interview feedback and a sample e-mail request can be downloaded at www.LegalJob.com/Resources.

CONCLUSION

Pulling It All Together

"If you always do what you've always done, you'll always get what you've always got." —Henry Ford

Having read this book, you will now have a strong sense of what you need to do to accelerate your career path and create multiple job opportunities. To assist you, here is a quick summary.

A Change in Perspective

An overall key to success is to shift your perspective from you to them. Instead of thinking like a law student seeking to be hired, put yourself mentally into the shoes of a future employer intent on fulfilling its mission. From this vantage point, the most important factor is not what you have accomplished and learned, but how your credentials can be used to help a potential employer overcome its challenges and realize its goals.

Making a Decision

Your next move is to formulate a plan and commit. This plan will provide tools for identifying, evaluating, and securing various opportunities, including those that are unforeseen. Your first step is to choose a major in a practice area where there is a need and you have some interest. When making this decision, do not waste time and energy thinking like a lawyer, hemming and hawing over your choices. Focus on what you want and why, and pick a major.

Taking Action

You have committed to a plan and a major. Now, you are ready to put your plan into action.

The first step is networking. When networking, be clear about your purpose and demonstrate an interest in the opinions, career path, and concerns of others.

The next action to take is to look at things from the employer's perspective when building your brand. You should use your resume, cover letter, and 30-second commercial to demonstrate that you have the skills, experience, results, and habits your dream employer is seeking.

Further connect your brand to an employer's need by becoming an expert on the employer. Becoming an expert involves obtaining a strong understanding of the employer's needs and objectives, demonstrating this understanding, and articulating how hiring you will be the best way for the employer to obtain the required results.

The key to successful execution is to focus on the plan and not the outcome. Successful candidates stay committed to their plan. They convert limiting thoughts and less-than-perfect outcomes into motivators. They also turn rejections into opportunities by seeking feedback and making any necessary changes.

◆ ◆ ◆

These strategies have helped many law students and law firm associates to secure their ideal legal job. If you have found the insights in this book helpful and want hands-on assistance to identify your desired job, create a clear plan for securing it, and quickly and completely execute the plan, then e-mail **adam@legaljob.com** for information about the "Accelerate Your Career Path" one-on-one coaching program. This coaching program provides participants with insight, strategy, guidance, and support in their efforts to achieve their goals. It is available to both law students seeking to secure their first job and associates considering a move to a different firm or position.

If you are a career counsellor, dean, or other law school administrator, whose law students would benefit from additional strategies and tactics relating to the subjects covered in this book, e-mail **adam@legaljob.com** for information on law student group training seminars.

BONUS

Looking to Land Your Dream Legal Job?

As a thank you for purchasing this book, I'd like to invite you to take advantage of a special NO COST, "Career Clarity," personal one-on-one coaching session where I'll help you:

- Create a crystal-clear vision for the kind of legal job you'd like to attract and the kind of career that would excite you and make you feel fulfilled.
- Uncover hidden challenges that may be sabotaging your job hunting efforts and your success with prospective employers.
- Leave the session renewed, recharged, and inspired to find your dream job now.

To schedule your Career Clarity coaching session, go to **www.legaljob.com/securedreamjob** where you will fill out a short questionnaire and provide contact information so I can set up the coaching call with you.

Made in the USA
Coppell, TX
19 December 2019

13414373R00069